ROUTE 66

SPIRIT OF THE MOTHER ROAD

BY BOB MOORE

NORTHLAND PUBLISHING

Passing through eight states and three time zones, Route 66, as displayed on a vintage Curt Teich postcard, exposes the roadie to 2,448 miles of real America.

TE
6

Chicago

"OF AMERICA"

TEST YOUR
CLASSIC CAR IQ

Throughout the book, you will find classic cars at the top of many pages. Test your knowledge and see how many you can identify. The answers can be found under the flap of the back cover.

INTRODUCTION

ROUTE 66 is arguably the most well known highway in the world. It is a 2,448-mile living museum open to any and all who possess the spirit of adventure and the desire to discover the real America. For over three-quarters of a century, Route 66 has fueled the passions of those who understand that a road is more than just a strip of concrete or asphalt. A road is the way out of town to someplace never before seen, an open-ended invitation to explore and find a new way of life.

Route 66 began as a dream in the early 1920s when Cyrus Avery, a savvy businessman, Oklahoma State Highway Commissioner, and member of the American Association of State Highway Officials, envisioned a road that would connect the upper Midwest with the riches of California (and pass through Tulsa in the process). After much debate, a decision was finally reached and on July 23, 1926, Route 66 officially opened up the way from Chicago to Los Angeles.

But soon, Route 66 became more than just the road of commerce connecting the Windy City with the ever-increasing market demands of the booming West Coast. As the Great Depression held the country in the grip of economic turmoil, a massive dust storm, beginning on May 10, 1934, blew an estimated 300 million tons of topsoil off the parched lands of Colorado, Kansas, Texas, and Oklahoma. Over the next five years, the winds blew and the sun became so obscured by the airborne dust

GAS 11½
TAXES 3 & 1

1-	.16
2-	.31
3-	.47
4-	.62
5-	.78
6-	.93
7-	1.09
8-	1.24
9-	1.40
10-	1.55
11-	1.71
12-	1.86
13-	2.02
14-	2.17
15-	2.33

that young children did not truly comprehend the difference between night and day. These were the years of the Dust Bowl, when tenant farmers lost their lands to banks and people took to the road in search of a better life—a better life promised by brightly colored flyers promoting jobs in the fields of California.

> "They come into 66 from the tributary side roads, from the wagon tracks and the rutted country roads. 66 is the mother road, the road of flight."
> —THE GRAPES OF WRATH

With those simple words, novelist John Steinbeck summed up the importance of Route 66 to those fleeing the Dust Bowl. And in the process, he gave a new name to the highway—Route 66 had become the Mother Road.

December 7, 1941 plunged the United States into World War II, and with the war came massive truck convoys and troop trains moving soldiers across the country. During these long years, travel on Route 66 nearly came to a stop. Gas and tires were rationed and the lack of new cars due to an automobile production shutdown, which lasted from 1942 until late 1945, kept the general public from traveling. For the most part, the people who were on the road were job seekers heading to the huge Kaiser steel mill in Fontana, CA, or to the new aircraft plants in Los Angeles and San Diego. The war years brought a profound change to the towns and the people along Route 66.

TOP: *Breakdowns were an everyday part of life for the Dust Bowl migrants traveling Route 66 to the golden land of California.* **LEFT:** *An early advertising card for Gulf Oil Company, founded in 1907. The company was bought by Chevron in 1984.* **ABOVE MIDDLE:** *Placards on gas pumps in the early 1940s, indicated the per-gallon price of gasoline plus Federal and State taxes.* **ABOVE:** *Gas station attendants proudly wore the company logo patch on all of their uniforms.*

> IT WINDS
> FROM CHICAGO TO L.A.,
> MORE THAN 2,000 MILES
> ALL THE WAY.
> GET YOUR KICKS…
> ON ROUTE 66!
>
> —BOBBY TROUP

RIGHT: *A classic road cruiser, the 1959 Cadillac Fleetwood.*
BELOW: *The Whiting Bros Motel in Yucca, AZ offered the unique enticement of a swimming pool.*

Finally, in 1945 when the war ended, thousands of G.I.s returned to the U.S., passing through California on the way home. And having seen the Golden State, they began dreaming of palm trees, clean air, modern homes, and an economy not based on steel mills or coal mines. So they returned home, gathered their young families, and set out for California along Route 66, the road that symbolized a new, more prosperous life.

The 1950s saw the dawn of a wealthy America, one with solid paychecks and leisure time unlike anything previously experienced. The new residents of California loaded their families into the giant behemoths of the road, celebrating the "Forward Look" of the new Chryslers or the "Swept-Wing" designs of General Motors. With these new vehicles, Route 66 became an icon for travel. Images of the road included roadside diners and cafés and motels with garish neon signs and inviting swimming pools. Trading Posts were a dream come true for visiting children, especially when the stop included the purchase of a rubber tomahawk, a beaded necklace, or a small box of local rocks. When the vacation was over, Route 66 comfortably led weary travelers home—home to California with its blue skies, new schools, and eternal feeling of optimism.

The 1960s brought Sunset Boulevard and Haight-Ashbury, along with sex, drugs, and rock-n-roll. Jimi, Janis, Jim, and Jefferson Airplane—they were all there, all on the coast. So California called once again, and the Love Generation piled into VW buses or stood by the roadside with thumbs pointing west, hoping for a ride that would take them all the way. Once again, Route 66 transplanted a generation of youth from farms, small towns, and the boredom of home to the land of excitement.

Recreational vehicle mania hit the nation during the 1970s, as retirees and hard working baby boomers alike took to the road in travel trailers, truck campers, and motor homes. The roadside changed slightly as KOA and other campground chains seemingly appeared overnight. But the gas crunch of the mid-'70s caught everyone off guard, and soon, long road trips were no longer the order of the day. Weekends closer to home changed travel in the United States. Route 66 businesses had seen hard times before, so they still had hope. They viewed the gas shortage as just another set-back until the next big boom would arrive. Unfortunately, the next big boom never came.

By the mid-1980s, Route 66 was officially dead. The government removed the signs, and the most memorable 2,448 miles of highway in the United States were no more. But dreams and memories do not die easily. Route 66 continued to live on in the memories of those who had traveled her and in the dreams of those who still wanted to experience the magic of the Mother Road. Anniversaries, honeymoons, family trips, and the search for the neon rainbow have since spurred the rebirth of the road. People from every country venture to Chicago and then continue west on Route 66 searching for the Gemini Giant, the bridge with the bend in the middle, Jessie James' hideout, ten Cadillacs buried in the Texas clay, a wigwam to sleep in, the vast depths of the Grand Canyon, the Great American Desert, and finally, the azure waters of the Pacific Ocean.

This is your invitation to embrace the Mother Road—stop at the mom and pop cafés for some real road food, visit the tourist traps that make a road trip memorable, and discover for yourself what it means to Get Your Kicks On Route 66!

ILLINOIS

LAND OF LINCOLN

OPPOSITE: *The proud statue welcomes guests to the Chicago Art Museum.*
TOP: *A portion of the old brick-paved Route 66 winds through farm fields south of Chicago.* RIGHT: *For the westbound roadie, Route 66 begins at the intersection of Adams Street and Michigan Avenue in downtown Chicago.* BELOW: *The heart of Chicago lies along Lake Michigan.*

FOR MOST PEOPLE, Route 66 conjures images of the wide-open spaces of the West, the small town atmosphere of the heartland, and rustic mom and pop cafés, but the start of a Route 66 trip actually begins buried deep in the concrete jungle of downtown Chicago. Originally, Route 66 began at the intersection of Harlem Avenue and Joliet Road in a suburb just outside of the city. In 1937, it was moved to the intersection of Lake Shore Drive and Jackson Drive. Years later, the streets were turned into one-way streets, and the journey now begins at Adams Street and Michigan Avenue. Take the turn heading westbound on Adams Street and begin the adventure of a lifetime.

Chicago was acquired from the Miami (my-am-uh) people in 1795 with the Treaty of Greenville. One of the first things the new residents did was to create a harbor in Lake Michigan for the new city. By 1825, the Erie Canal was complete and with it came an easy passage from Buffalo, New York. Thousands of people migrated from Buffalo to Chicago in 1833, beginning a surge that would last for years. By the mid-1850s, Chicago had grown to cover eighteen square-miles, and as the railroads pushed westward, Chicago became a major rail center for the grain and livestock markets, soon eclipsing New Orleans as a primary shipping point for grain, hogs, and cattle. Today, Chicago is the nation's third largest city with a population approaching three million. It is still a major rail and trucking center, has two airports, and over two-dozen major colleges and universities, including Northwestern University, University of Chicago, University of Illinois at Chicago, DePaul University, and Illinois Institute of Technology.

Historic Route 66 signs lead the way out of the industrial areas of the city through Cicero, Berwyn, and Joliet, passing Statesville Prison in the process. And in case you were wondering, that is not the home of Jake and Elwood Blues, better known as the Blues Brothers. Their home was in Joliet Prison, just a few blocks off Route 66.

Suddenly, the city is left behind as the road enters farm country and the small towns of central Illinois. By avoiding the interstate, it is possible to travel for miles on the old highway, visiting numerous small towns that harken back to a much simpler and slower paced America—back to a time when every town square had a bandstand and the local café was the place to be on Friday night.

As you approach the town of Wilmington, a giant green spaceman looms to the right. It is the 20-foot-tall Gemini Giant, the "greeter" for the Launching Pad Drive-In since 1965. No trip along 66 would be complete without a picture taken next to this Route 66 icon.

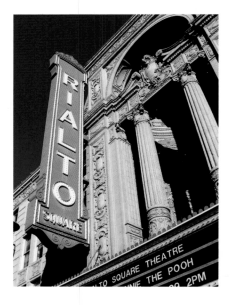

ABOVE: *The classic Rialto Theatre in downtown Chicago.* **BELOW:** *An early 1900s view of the Chicago Art Museum with bustling traffic on Michigan Avenue. Notice the traffic control booth (lower right) high above the vehicles.*

Not fast food, but good food cooked to order is the name of the game at the Launching Pad.

Pass through Dwight, and follow the road south. Here, you can still see one of the few remaining barn advertisements for the Meramec Caverns in Stanton, Missouri.

Pontiac is home to the Old Log Cabin Restaurant, a testament to the determination of a Route 66 business. The original road, which can still be seen behind the building, used to run prominently past the restaurant's entrance. When the new four-lane was built, the owners actually jacked up the building and rotated it 180 degrees so that the front of the restaurant would face the new highway.

Lexington offers a wonderful section of the old highway, complete with classic billboards and Burma Shave signs. During the Taste of Country Fair and Route 66 Reunion, held the fourth weekend in July each year, this section of the old highway becomes Memory Lane and attracts photographers from all over the world.

The road south of Bloomington, where the original Illinois Republican Party was formed, leads to a sweet stop. Funks Grove is the home of pure Maple Sirup. (Yes, "sirup." This spelling indicates there is no sugar added.) The Funk family has been tapping maples since the late 1800s, and each year when Funks Grove Pure Maple Sirup hits the shelves, it is a sure sign that spring is not far behind.

A slow pace is the order of the day with visits to McLean, Atlanta, Lincoln, Broadwell, and Williamsville. Atlanta is a quiet town with a wonderful octagonal shaped museum, formerly the town library. Lincoln is the only town to bear the former president's name with his consent, although he did comment, "I never knew anything named Lincoln that amounted to much."

Broadwell is not much more than a wide spot in the road with a few grain elevators, but it can boast that it is the site of Ernie Edwards' Pig Hip Restaurant, a Route 66 icon from 1937 until Ernie retired in 1992. In its prime, it was known far and wide for serving the best pork along the road; all it took was the enticing aroma wafting across the highway to stop hungry travelers. Today, the Pig Hip is being restored as a museum.

Williamsville is one of the most attractive small towns on this stretch of Route 66. A nice, down-home café is in the center of town and the atmosphere around the city park makes for a quiet respite from the road.

TOP RIGHT: *An entrant in the annual Solar Challenge passes the Gemini Giant in Bloomington.*
MIDDLE RIGHT: *Ernie and Francis Edwards pose outside of the historic Pig Hip Restaurant in Broadwell.*
BOTTOM RIGHT: *Although bypassed by the interstate in 1976, Funk's Grove continues to supply sweet maple "sirup" to a host of dedicated fans around the world.*

Chicago is a city that lives and breathes music. From jazz to the blues, the city rumbles with the newest sounds, innovations, and historic rhythms of America.

After World War I, Chicago and other northern cities saw the arrival of an estimated one million African Americans, all searching for a brighter future. With them came the first sweet sounds of the blues. Early blues artists such as Blind Lemon Jefferson and Alberta Hunter quickly moved in and started spreading their sound.

The 1940s and '50s saw a slight restructuring in the blues as amplification, rhythm sections, and guitar leads combined with the sound of the Mississippi Delta, giving birth to modern-day blues. Overnight, new recording studios popped up, bringing forth the first-generation of true Chicago blues artists. Muddy Waters, Little Walter, Howlin' Wolf, Willie Dixon, and Bo Diddley created music that would go on to influence great bands like The Rolling Stones, the Blues Brothers, and even the Beatles. Today, few cities can match Chicago for the blues. Good places to relax and hear true Chicago blues are B.L.U.E.S. at 2519 N. Halsted and Buddy Guy's Legends at 754 S. Wabash Avenue.

The Chicago jazz scene was born in 1917 with the closing of the Storyville district in New Orleans. Jazz artists left the dying city in search of new venues, and many of them found Chicago to be a suitable home. Earl "Fatha" Hines, Jelly Roll Morton, and Frankie Jaxon were the first to establish the jazz scene in the city. Over the years, Jazz moved from the Dixieland sound to pure jazz to what is known as the smooth jazz of today. Jazz still thrives in Chicago and cool licks can be heard at the Green Mill at 4802 N. Broadway (a 1930s Capone hangout); The Bop Shop at 1443 W. Jarvis Avenue; and Joe's Be-Bop Café and Jazz Emporium at 11 E. Hubbard Street.

OPPOSITE: *Bo Diddley and his Mean Machine brought a mixture of Rhythm & Blues, Rock, and down-home Blues to Chicago.*
RIGHT: *Abraham Lincoln's home in Springfield is now a historic site maintained by the National Park Service.* **BELOW LEFT:** *The Ariston Café in Litchfield has been a Route 66 dining tradition for over 75 years.*
BELOW RIGHT: *The Illinois State Capitol Building, Springfield.*

The next town on the route is Sherman, and then you enter Springfield. When Illinois was admitted to the Union in 1818, there was no Springfield, but by 1821, it was the county seat of Sangammon County. And in 1837, with the help of a young lawyer named Abraham Lincoln, it became the State Capital. Lincoln remained in Springfield until he was elected president of the United States in 1861. The Lincoln Home, now maintained by the National Park Service, was purchased by Lincoln in 1844 and was the only home ever owned by the former president.

Continuing south, Route 66 crosses into the southern Illinois coal-mining district, a huge area that encompasses six counties. Litchfield is a bustling community and the home of the Ariston Café, a family owned business since 1924. A stop at this restaurant is a true roadie tradition, as you will be rewarded with good food in a fine atmosphere.

Mt. Olive was the center of coal mining and union activities in the late 1800s and the final resting place of Mary Harris, more popularly known as Mother Jones, a fierce fighter for the rights of miners and children. Her simple headstone is at the base of a tall monument in the Union Miner's Cemetery. Mt. Olive is also the site of Soulsby's Station, operated from 1926 until the mid-'90s by brother and sister Russell and Ola Soulsby. Atypical for the times, the station not only sold gasoline, but ice cream bars and other snacks as well. For a few years during the 1930s, there was even a slot machine bolted to the counter top until a thief broke in and pried it loose. Outside is an old car lube rack, unused for so many years a tree now grows through the center of it. Soulsby's, being high on the list of Route 66 icons, was recently restored by the Illinois Route 66 Association.

Continue south through Staunton and Hamel. In Hamel, look for St. Paul Lutheran Church. At the top of this classic church is the Neon Cross of Route 66—a beacon for Route 66 travelers for nearly sixty years.

At Edwardsville you begin the descent onto the eastern edge of the American Bottom, an area that has been technically classified as being "as flat as a table top."

Brilliant colors, fantastic shapes, and smooth animation are a few of the reasons neon signs gained in popularity. Combined with the fact that a neon sign can be seen at a distance of ten times that of a conventional sign makes it a natural fit for the roadside business owner.

Neon, from the Greek word neos, meaning "the new gas," is the name given to the labor-intensive process of hand-bending glass tubes into specific designs. The basic colors created are the result of the type of gas inside the tube: blue—argon enhanced with mercury, white—carbon dioxide, gold—helium, red—neon gas. Other colors are the result of various phosphor coatings inside the tube.

Neon signs were invented by French engineer and chemist Georges Claude in 1902. He displayed the new concept to the public on December 11, 1910 in Paris.

The first neon signs in America were sold by Claude's company in 1923 to Earl C. Anthony, a Los Angeles, California, Packard automobile dealer. The two signs with the word "PACKARD" cost $12,000 each, which is equivalent to nearly $127,000 today. Dubbed "liquid fire," people would stop and stare at these first examples of what would become one of the most widely used materials for signage in the world.

From here you cross the bottomland, following the Historic Route 66 signs to the Chain of Rocks Road and Mitchell. Many older motels dot the stretch of road through Mitchell, each bearing great old neon signs, still used to entice the traveler from the road. Continue west on the Chain of Rocks Road to the Chain of Rocks Bridge.

The Chain of Rocks Bridge was built in 1929 and financed by tolls. Originally, the bridge was designed to go straight across the river, like a normal bridge, and connect Illinois and Missouri. But the two states were in such a hurry to get the bridge completed that they started building from both sides of the river. When they were nearing the middle, they realized they were a day late and a dollar short—there wasn't any bedrock in that section of the river to build a solid foundation. To remedy the situation, they finished the bridge about 200 yards up river. Because of this poor planning, the bridge has a 22-degree bend in the middle, making it one of the most architecturally interesting bridges ever constructed. At a little over one mile in length, the bridge is the longest pedestrian bridge in the world and offers a great view of the Mississippi River. After the bridge was closed in 1969, it was used in the film "Escape From New York." Watch for it towards the end of the film.

Your cross-country journey has now taken you through the scenic back roads and small towns of Illinois—but there is much more to see. Continue on over the Missouri state line and venture farther along the Mother Road.

TOP: *St. Paul Lutheran Church in Hamel and its famous neon cross.* **ABOVE:** *Neon signs like this one light the way for travelers all across the country.* **LEFT:** *The Chain of Rocks Bridge crosses the Mississippi River just north of St. Louis.*

CHICAGO

The Art Institute of Chicago
111 S. Michigan Avenue
312.443.3600, www.artic.edu
The world's most impressive collection of impressionist and
post-impressionist art

Museum of Broadcast Communications
78 E. Washington (in the Chicago Cultural Center)
312.629.6000, www.museum.tv/
History of broadcasting with interactive displays and archives
of programming

Lincoln Park
2001 N. Clark Street
312.742.2000, www.lpzoo.com
Largest park in the city, contains the Conservatory and the
Lincoln Park Zoo

Museum of Science and Industry
57th Street and S. Lakeshore Drive
773.684.1414, www.msichicago.org
Largest science museum in a single building in the Western
Hemisphere and the first museum to develop the idea of
hands-on interactive exhibits

Navy Pier
600 E. Grand Avenue
312.595.7437, www.navypier.com
Botanical Garden, IMAX theatre, Chicago Children's Museum,
retail shops, and sightseeing cruises

Sears Tower Skydeck
233 S. Wacker Drive
312.675.9696, www.the-skydeck.com
The tallest building in the United States at 1,353 feet offers
spectacular views of the city.

SPRINGFIELD

The Dana-Thomas House
300 E. Lawrence Avenue
217.782.6776, www.dana-thomas.org
First prairie-style home designed by Frank Lloyd Wright,
built in 1904

Lincoln Home National Historic Site
413 S. Eighth Street
217.492.4241 ext.221, www.nps.gov/liho
The only home Lincoln ever owned is the centerpiece of a
four-square-block neighborhood that is being restored to the
look of the mid-1800s.

*Once a small army post, Lincoln
Park, located 2 1/2 miles from
downtown Chicago, is a progressive
neighborhood recognized for its wide
array of entertainment, dining,
culture, and recreational activities.*

MISSOURI

THE SHOW ME STATE

ROUTE 66 ACROSS MISSOURI brings the beauty of the Ozarks, the hideout of Jesse James, and wonderful old sections of the road that are dedicated to the slower pace of days gone by.

The 630-foot high stainless steel Gateway Arch is the centerpiece of the National Expansion Memorial Park, welcoming Route 66 visitors to St. Louis. The park was established in 1935 to commemorate the westward growth of the United States. Construction of the Gateway Arch, designed by architect Eero Saarinen, began in 1963 and was completed in 1966. A unique tram system allows visitors to ride to the top of the arch and enjoy spectacular views of the Mississippi River and the city.

The first settlement in the St. Louis area was the Jesuit Mission of St. Francis Xavier in 1700 at the mouth of the Rivière des Pères (River of the Fathers). The mission was abandoned within three years, and it took another sixty years before a New Orleans-based fur trading company was granted rights to trade in the Missouri River Valley. In February of 1764, the St. Louis town site was laid out. Named for Louis IX, Crusader King of France and patron saint of Louis XV, St. Louis began to prosper. Throughout its history, St. Louis grew from a small-time fur trading town to one of the most important shipping points in the United States. By 1880, there were over 350,000 people in St. Louis, and the steady steamboat traffic moved St. Louis into the position of being the largest town in the U.S. west of Pittsburgh.

Railroads, steamships, and wagon trains kept St. Louis at the forefront of American progress through the late 1800s, and by 1904, the city was ready to celebrate. To the tune of "Meet me in St. Louis, Louis, meet me at the Fair," people flocked to the Louisiana Purchase Exposition and were introduced to the hot dog, ice cream cone, and iced tea.

OPPOSITE: *The graceful Gateway Arch in National Expansion Memorial Park in St. Louis can be seen from all over the city.*

TOP: *A pair of barns sport classic Meramec Caverns signs alongside Route 66.* **RIGHT:** *Putting the sky-high finishing touches on the Gateway Arch in 1966, as seen from East St. Louis.*

The first International Balloon Race was held in St. Louis in 1908, and twenty years later, thanks to the financial backing of local businessmen, Charles Lindbergh flew solo across the Atlantic in a plane named The Spirit of St. Louis. Today, the aircraft industry is still a major player in the St. Louis area with Boeing Aircraft being a major employer.

With all of its wonderful history, St. Louis offers the Route 66 traveler enough attractions that a two or three day visit is a must. For the roadie in search of true Route 66 experiences, St. Louis is a treasure, offering the culinary delights of Ted Drewes Custard Stand on west Chippewa Street—be sure to try a concrete milkshake—to the racy history of the Coral Court Motel. The Coral Court Motel was a classic "no-tell Route 66 motel," and after its demolition, it became the first motel in the nation to have a book written about it: *Tales From the Coral Court* by Shellee Graham.

And while you'll hate to leave the sites and thrills of the big city, there is so much more to see. So continue west to the Route 66 State Park and Museum. The 419-acre park houses Route 66 memorabilia and interprets the environmental success story of the former resort community of Times Beach, which once thrived on the location of the park.

Forging on, Route 66 passes through numerous other small town locales. Pacific, St. Clair, and Stanton are the sites of many great tourist attractions. The Antique Toy Museum hosts a collection of over 3,000 antique and collectible toy tractors, cars, trucks, trains, dolls, and doll house furniture dating from 1928 to 1964. The Jesse James Museum is dedicated to the presumption that the famed outlaw did not die in 1882 in St. Joseph, Missouri, but lived on until 1952.

Three and half miles south of Stanton are Meramec Caverns. Opened in 1935, Meramec

was the first major cave discovered on the North American continent and contains more than 26 miles of underground passages. The tour takes you through a mile of caverns all registering a pleasant 60°F.

Continuing on Route 66, you pass through hill country and into Rolla, Missouri's grape-growing region. From here, Route 66 enters the Ozarks, one of the oldest mountain ranges in North America. With over 4,000 caves in the region, it is little wonder that Missouri is known as the Cave State. Homesteaders, who moved into the region looking for better land, settled the area following the Civil War. The feisty sounds of fiddle music soon filled the hills. Today, that sweet bluegrass sound has swept music lovers across the nation.

ABOVE: *The Coral Court Motel, a streamline modern classic in St. Louis.* **LEFT:** *Step back in time to when toy trucks were made of steel and Howdy Doody puppets were all the rage at the Antique Toy Museum in Stanton.* **BOTTOM:** *Colored lights highlight the natural beauty within Meramec Caverns, as well as the hideout of the notorious Jesse James.* **OPPOSITE:** *Charles Lindbergh standing proudly in front of the famous Spirit of St. Louis.*

ST. LOUIS

Jefferson National Expansion Memorial

11 N. 4th Street

314.655.1700, www.nps.gov/jeff

A national park covering the site of the St. Louis settlement and dedicated to commemorating the westward expansion of the United States

The Gateway Arch

St. Louis Riverfront

877.982.1410, www.stlouisarch.com

Take the tram to the top, 630 feet above the riverfront, for an awe-inspiring view of the city and the Mississippi River.

The Magic House, St. Louis Children's Museum

516 S. Kirkwood Road

314.822.8900, www.magichouse.com

This is an award-winning children's museum.

Museum of Transportation

3015 Barrett Station Road

314.965.7998, www.museumoftransport.org

Buses, trains (more than 70 locomotives), cars, and a restored section of the Coral Court Motel

STANTON

Meramec Caverns

I-44 West, Exit 230

800.676.6105, www.americascave.com

Five floors of colorful mineral displays plus the hideout of Jesse James

ROLLA

Memoryville, USA

2220 N. Bishop Avenue

573.364.1810, www.memoryvilleusa.com

Cars from 1907 to the present, plus an auto restoration shop and art gallery

SPRINGFIELD

American National Fish and Wildlife Museum

500 W. Sunshine Street

417.890.9453, www.wondersofwildlife.org

An amazing museum devoted to the wonders of the great outdoors of America

Fantastic Caverns

4872 N. Farm Road 125

417.833.2010, www.fantasticcaverns.com

Take a tram tour through one of Missouri's largest caves.

OPPOSITE: *The vivid neon sign of the Munger Moss Motel welcomes weary travelers.* **TOP:** *Built of native stone, the Jasper County Courthouse in Carthage is one of the premier show-places of the city.* **ABOVE:** *John's Modern Cabins east of Arlington are a preservation project of Missouri's Friends of the Mother Road.* **RIGHT:** *Topiary beasts watch over the Mother Road as it winds through the Devil's Elbow area.*

Following Old Route 66, you'll pass through the massive Hooker Cut, the last section of Old 66 to be replaced in Missouri. This section of road, which was cut deeply out of solid rock, is a true testament to the art of road construction. Just ahead is Devil's Elbow, located in an area that the Missouri State Planning Commission calls one of the seven beauty spots in Missouri. Devil's Elbow, a severe bend in the Big Piney River, was given the name by lumberjacks, who constantly fought log-jams at this sharp curve in the river. They claimed that the boulder causing the bend must have been placed there by the devil.

From the river, the road climbs the bluffs and offers spectacular views of the Big Piney River and the surrounding hill country. The road winds its way down and travels through Waynesville, Hazelgreen, and on to Lebanon.

Lebanon was named for Lebanon, Tennessee, the original home of many of the town's settlers. On the east side of town is the Munger Moss Motel, a long time roadie favorite. The Munger Moss has a grand tradition of serving Route 66 travelers, dating back to the time before the Munger Moss Motel even existed. The original roadie attraction was a tiny barbecue café operated by Mr. and Mrs. Munger at Devil's Elbow. When Mr. Munger passed on, Nellie Munger remarried Emmet Moss, and the place became Munger Moss Barbecue. Eventually, a couple by the name of Hudson bought the café and kept the business booming until the early 1940s, when the Devil's Elbow section of Route 66 was realigned and the café was no longer on the main road. To remedy this situation, the Hudson's decided to purchase a new piece of property that was located closer to the new highway. By 1946, the Munger Moss Motel was built and opened with four-teen cabins. Today, Bob and Ramona Lehman, who bought the motel in 1971, still labor long hours to ensure that the roadies of the world have a "Home Away From Home."

The steep hills give way to a more rolling topography as Route 66 makes its way west past Conway, Marshfield, and then into the bustling city of Springfield. Missouri's third largest city, Springfield was founded by John Polk Campbell in 1830 at a site then known as Kickapoo Prairie. Campbell went on to become the county clerk, and he donated fifty acres of land for the town site. Soon Springfield was a busy little town with many of its own successful industries.

Outside of Springfield, Route 66 travels virtually straight through Plano, Halltown, Albatross, Rescue, Log City, Stone City, and Avilla before crossing the Spring River and entering Carthage, the site of one of the most photographed courthouses in the country. It is a true architectural wonder, and something not to miss. From Carthage, it is a short trip through Webb City and Joplin, a city that sits atop a labyrinth of mine tunnels, now filled with water to support the city above.

The trip across Missouri touched on beautiful and wild country, but now the Mother Road begins to plummet as she heads for the great American West. Huge cities like St. Louis and Chicago lie behind you and will not be experienced again until you reach Los Angeles. Head west on Old Route 66, and within a few miles, you'll cross into Kansas.

KANSAS

THE SUNFLOWER STATE

The Galena Museum is a small gem that should not be missed. Housed in the former MKT railway depot, the museum offers mementos from the heyday of Galena, along with railroad and Route 66 memorabilia dating from the early 1900s.

The next town on the route is Riverton, the home of the Kansas Historic Route 66 Association. Also in Riverton is Eisler Bros., a classic general store and a great stop for Route 66 souvenirs and a snack. Opened in 1925, Eisler Bros. has served the public with friendly service that is always backed by a smile. Store owner Scott Nelson is always glad to greet the traveling roadie, so when you stop by, be sure to sign the guest book and marvel at the thousands of people from all over the world who have signed before you.

Between Riverton and Baxter Springs is the only remaining Marsh Arch, or Rainbow Bridge on Route 66. This unique design by James Marsh used a complex steel skeleton encased in concrete with the bridge deck suspended from the concrete and steel arches.

ROUTE 66 CLIPS the southeastern corner of Kansas for only thirteen miles, and in the process, it passes through an historic area of the United States. In the late 1870s, Galena, Kansas, was the site of massive lead mines, and in the space of two months, over 3,000 people moved to the area, giving the town a Wild West reputation. To the north, the "respectable" residents of Empire City decided that they did not want the unlawful atmosphere of Galena to adversely affect their community, so a large log wall was built between the two cities to help ensure the sanctity of Empire City. The citizens of Galena watched with interest as the wall was painstakingly constructed, and when it was finished, the residents of Galena promptly burned it to the ground.

OPPOSITE: *Fields of brilliant yellow sunflowers welcome you to Kansas.*
TOP: *The last remaining Marsh Arch, or Rainbow Bridge, on Route 66.*
MIDDLE: *Eisler Bros. Old Country Store has provided friendly service to roadies for over 75 years.*

**GET YOUR KICKS
ON ROUTE 66!**

If you ever plan to motor west,
Travel my way; take the highway that's the best.
Get your kicks on Route 66!

It winds from Chicago to L. A.
More than 2000 miles all the way.
Get your kicks on Route 66!

Now you go thru St. Louie, Joplin, Missouri,
And Oklahoma City is mighty pretty.
You'll see Amarillo, Gallup, New Mexico,
Flagstaff, Arizona, don't forget Winona,
Kingman, Barstow, San Bernardino.

Won't you get hip to this timely tip,
When you make that California trip.
Get your kicks on Route 66!

— Bobby Troup (1918-1999)

Marsh built hundreds of these bridges in the 1910s-1930s. This bridge was threatened with destruction in the early 1990s, but the Kansas Historic Route 66 Association and roadies from around the world petitioned the state to save it. A new bridge was built, but the Marsh Arch was saved.

Baxter Springs prides itself as being "The First Cowtown in Kansas" with a history dating back to the 1860s. Each summer, Texas cattlemen would drive thousands of longhorns to the area to feed on the abundant grasslands of eastern Kansas. With the arrival of the railroad, the cowboys began taking their cattle to places like Wichita and Dodge City, where they could easily meet the train and transport their cattle back East for sale. But even though Baxter Springs lost the adventure of the annual cattle drives, it quickly settled back into life as a quiet farming community. Today, as you pass through town on your way across Route 66, you will be greeted with friendly smiles and tales of days gone by.

In a short thirteen miles, you have crossed Kansas. Ahead lies Oklahoma, and once across the state line, Route 66 will begin moving into the Great American West.

OPPOSITE: *Famous jazz artist, Bobby Troup, and his lovely wife, Julie London, in a late 1960s portrait. Bobby Troup went on to write the famous lyrics "Get Your Kicks on Route 66!"*

ABOVE: *The Galena Museum is housed in the classic M-K-T (Missouri-Kansas-Texas) depot.*

BELOW: *Roadies will see Historic Route 66 signs like this one scattered across all eight states.*

OKLAHOMA

THE SOONER STATE

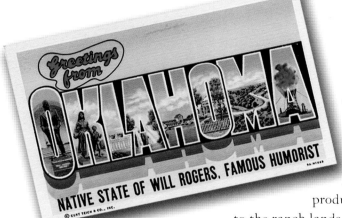

OPPOSITE: *The beautiful fall colors near Sapulpa Creek County offer a warm welcome to Oklahoma.* **TOP:** *The nine-foot wide Sidewalk Highway still carries traffic outside of Miami, OK.* **ABOVE RIGHT:** *The beautifully restored Coleman Theatre in Miami.* **BOTTOM:** *The boyhood home of baseball great Mickey Mantle is located on Mickey Mantle Blvd. in Commerce. The home is being restored by the Oklahoma Route 66 Association.*

THE TRIP ACROSS THE Sooner State is going to be an adventure, taking you from the grasslands of the east through the oil-producing region in the middle to the ranch lands of the west.

Entering from Kansas, the road passes through an area where large mounds rise alongside the highway. These are piles of chat, debris left over from the zinc mining that was once the primary industry here. Underground is part of an abandoned lead mine that produced over $10 million in lead, which is equivalent to $215 million today.

The quiet little town of Quapaw welcomes you to Oklahoma with a series of wonderful murals depicting old roadside scenes from an earlier age. The murals decorate many of the buildings in town and provide for some great photographic opportunities.

Ahead is Miami. Nope—you said it wrong—it is a Native American word and is pronounced *my-am-uh*. The town was named in honor of the Miami Indian tribe. Downtown is the beautifully restored Coleman Theatre, which originally opened in April of 1929 as The Coleman Theatre Beautiful.

South of Miami is the famous Sidewalk Highway, a roadway only nine feet wide. It was built in 1922, and there are countless stories about why this stretch of road is so narrow. The one I like the best claims that the road between Miami and Afton needed to be paved, but there was only enough money to pave it half way. Local leaders decided that if they paved it half as wide as a normal road, they could pave it all the way. True story or local legend? Who knows, but it makes for a great story. This is a rough section of road, but drivable. You can bypass this amazing stretch of road, but why miss the adventure?

Next, you'll come to Afton, a small town with some fine old buildings, gas stations, and abandoned motor courts. Be sure to stop at Afton Station and see Laurel Kane, who has one of the largest Route 66 postcard collections along the road.

The names slowly pass by—Vinita, White Oak, Chelsea, Bushyhead, and Foyil, where you have the opportunity to see some real Oklahoma folk art at the Totem Pole Park. The totem poles in the park were created by Ed Galloway as a tribute to local Native Americans. The totems were constructed between 1940 and 1948, and during this time, Galloway earned the honor of building the world's largest totem pole at 90 feet. Foyil is also home to Andy Payne, a runner who won the 1928 Bunion Derby—a transcontinental footrace from Los Angeles to New York City, most of which was run along Route 66. A statue honoring his victory stands tall in the park at the west end of town.

Continuing on down the road is Claremore, the hometown of Will Rogers and the site of the Will Rogers Memorial Museum. Across the Verdigris River and on the right is the

Blue Whale, built in the late 1960s by Hugh Davis as a private water park for his family. The enormous Blue Whale has become a Route 66 icon. Restoration of the property allows you to visit this historic giant.

Following the road through Catoosa, Route 66 continues to Tulsa. Tulsa was settled in 1836, and with the arrival of the railroad in 1882, it quickly became a major shipping point for cattle. In 1901, however, Tulsa's future changed gears as black gold was discovered in the region and the title of the New Oil Capital of the Nation was secured. There was so much success and prosperity that Hollywood even made a movie about it in later years. "Tulsa" starring Susan Hayward, Robert Preston, and Chill Wills became the hit film of 1949.

West of Tulsa the road passes through the small town of Sapulpa, and just beyond is a chance to experience an old section of the road. Watch for the Ozark Trail sign on the west side of Sapulpa, make a right, and cross the brick-paved Rock Creek Bridge, a gorgeous place to stop and take a photo. Take your time as you follow the old highway for three miles through an over-hanging mantle of trees. Rolling hills and charming small

LEFT: *The Blue Whale at Catoosa, a classic icon of the road.*
BELOW LEFT: *The historic birthplace of Will Rogers near Oologah.*
BOTTOM: *For five years, the winds scoured the earth forcing people from their homes and farms across Oklahoma.* **BELOW RIGHT:** *The world's largest totem pole stands just outside of Foyil.*

TOP: *The Oklahoma Land Rush opened the Sooner State for settlement and gave the state its nickname.*
ABOVE: *The brick-paved Rock Creek Bridge west of Sapulpa.*
BOTTOM: *The unique beauty of the Round Barn in Arcadia is a must-see attraction.*

towns like Bristow and Depew provide life to the Mother Road between Tulsa and Oklahoma City.

Chandler is an example of one of America's "tough towns." A tornado in 1897 destroyed virtually every building in the community and killed fourteen people. Within days, the people rebounded and reconstruction of the town began. Years later, Chandler saw the last of the Old West gunfights, as Lawman Bill Tilghman was murdered in the streets.

West of Chandler stands the Seaba Station, originally opened as the Nevr Nox gas station in 1923. In 1995, the building was purchased by Sonny and Sue Preston, who have done an incredible amount of restoration. Today, the Seaba Station is listed on the National Register of Historic Places and is one of the premier antique shops along the road.

The Round Barn is an outstanding feature of Arcadia. Built by local farmer William Odor in 1898, the barn has been restored and is now a museum. Constructed out of burr oak that was soaked in the Deep Fork River and then bent into shape, the Round Barn, at 60 feet across and 43 feet in height, is an imposing sight along Route 66.

As the road continues west, the encroachment of the suburbs becomes evident with new road construction, housing developments, and the inevitable arrival of highway clutter. Oklahoma City has the distinction of having the only state capital building on Route 66 (on the 1938–1954 alignment).

Some towns claim to have "sprung up overnight," but Oklahoma City did it in thirty minutes. On April 22, 1889, at high noon, the signal was given to start the great Oklahoma land rush, and within fifteen minutes men from the Seminole Land and Town Company were dragging survey chains towards the site of Oklahoma City. How did everyone get there so fast since the starting line was tens of miles away? In anticipation of the amount of fertile land available, over a thousand people had illegally snuck across the starting lines and camped out along the Santa Fe railroad track near the projected town site. This early preparation spawned the nickname "sooner" and quickly led to Oklahoma being called the Sooner State.

The discovery of oil in 1928 forced a change in Oklahoma City. The once quiet, laid back town suddenly emerged as a bustling boomtown. Over 1,000 oil derricks were scattered across the city pumping that rich black gold. In the mid-1930s, one well, the Mary Sudik, more commonly known as Wild Mary, blew out its well casing. For eleven straight days, Wild Mary spewed a total of 110,000 gallons of oil into the air, covering homes, businesses, livestock, and people.

Continuing west, Yukon is easy to spot because of the huge grain elevators with "Yukon's Best Flour" painted on them. But that is not Yukon's most recent claim to fame. Yukon is also the home of country singing legend Garth Brooks.

El Reno is the next town on Route 66, and just west are verdant green fields, open vistas, and the first of many stretches of original 1932–1933 Portland concrete cement paving. Stark blue skies, large white clouds, and endless rolling hills come to life. Ahead, there is still the adventure of Route 66, but for now, the wide-open spaces

around the original roadway will take your breath away.

Soon you will come to the Pony Bridge. This bridge is 3,944 feet long and crosses the Canadian River on 38 beams or pony trusses. This impressive bridge was completed in 1933, and is still the second longest vintage bridge existing on Route 66.

To the north of Hinton Junction is the virtual ghost town of Bridgeport, a Route 66 town that was active in the 1920s and 1930s. When the road was realigned in the late 30s, the town slowly died. But the way local legend tells it is much more interesting. Old locals say the newspaper in Geary insisted that everyone in Bridgeport leave town because it was going to be a ghost town. So the residents of Bridgeport did just that, and now it is a ghost town.

Follow the uneven, curvy road to Hydro, where you'll find Lucille's Historic Route 66, an icon from the glory years. Lucille Hamons was known as the mother of the Mother Road. For over fifty years, Lucille's was the place to stop for a cold drink, some conversation, and maybe, just maybe, a helping hand when your car quit and everything seemed to be going against you. Pause for a moment, take a photo, and say "thanks" to a lady who made the Mother Road a special place.

TOP: *The Field of Chairs Memorial at St. Joseph's Church pays homage to the lives lost in the Oklahoma City tragedy.* **ABOVE:** *The William P. Murray Bridge, also known as The Pony Bridge, across the Canadian River near Bridgeport.*

LEFT: *Lucille's Historic Route 66 at Hydro, home to Lucille Hamons, the mother of the Mother Road.*

OPPOSITE: *The West became popular due, in large part, to these American icons Roy Rogers, The King of the Cowboys, with his horse Trigger (left) and William "Hopalong Cassidy" Boyd (right).*

AN AMERICAN LEGEND
By John R. Erickson

The American cowboy has become one of the most recognizable characters in world mythology. Show citizens of Japan, France, or Germany a wide-brimmed felt hat or a pair of high-topped boots with stacked heels, and they will likely say, "cowboy," and then "the West."

The cowboy entered the popular imagination in the 1870s and 1880s, when young cowpunchers began appearing as heroic characters in dime novels. Some of the earliest silent movies featured gun-toting cowboys, who righted wrongs and saved damsels in distress. By the 1940s, some of the cowboys were carrying guitars as well as six-shooters, and a flood of televisions westerns in the early 1950s made Gene Autry, Roy Rogers, and Hopalong Cassidy almost as famous as Dwight Eisenhower.

Such a magical cloud has gathered around the cowboy that it is easy to wonder, were there ever any real cowboys, and are they still around?

The answer to both questions is yes, and by following Route 66 deeper into the West, the opportunity to run into one of these legends increases with each passing mile.

If a single word could define this true American icon, it would be work. The cowboy was and is defined by his work, and the working cowboy is the root from which all of the others have sprung. Today, as in years past, he lives a fairly adventurous life, spends more time with animals than with humans, and is highly skilled and poorly paid for it. He still makes his living on horseback and carries a rope, but unlike the glorified TV version, he's not likely to be packing either a gun or a guitar.

The modern cowboy still holds a mythical status for many, but in reality, the American cowboy is just another man—one who has been blessed with heroic tendencies and honored with the peace and quiet of a solitary lifestyle.

The names begin piling up again: Clinton, which is home to the Oklahoma Route 66 Museum, Foss, Canute, and Elk City. In 1901, present-day Elk City was known as Busch in hopes of luring St. Louis beer magnate, Adolphus Busch, to the community to build a brewery. This was not a popular idea among the more temperate townsfolk, and when he arrived by train, angry citizens threatened to push a tall ladder onto the brew master. Fortunately, the protesters diffused their anger long enough to explain that a brewery was not wanted, and Mr. Busch quickly took his business elsewhere.

Officially renamed in 1907, Elk City has long been a favored overnight stop for Route 66 travelers, as it maintains a friendly atmosphere. While in town, don't miss the Old Town Museum complex, which is also the site of the National Route 66 Museum.

Ahead lies Sayre, a town many will recognize from the John Ford film classic "The Grapes of Wrath." Main Street and the courthouse were used in the film, although most people believe they are seeing the state capitol building in Oklahoma City.

The town of Erick—childhood home to singers Roger Miller and Sheb Wooley—is the site of the 100TH Meridian. This important geographic line might not mean much these days, but this little dividing line meant

life and death to many farmers living in the mid- to late-1800s. At that time, banks would not loan money to farmers west of the 100TH Meridian as everyone considered that to be the start of the great American desert. After all, who can farm in the desert?

Erick is also the home of Harley and Annabelle Russell, the self-proclaimed Mediocre Music Makers and operators of the Sand Hills Curiosity Shop. I can honestly declare from first-hand experience that these are two of the most fun-loving people along the Mother Road.

Texola is our final stop in Oklahoma. Just like all the other little towns along the route, Texola became a ghost town when I-40 diverted the local traffic. Old buildings, a tiny jail, and abandoned gas stations are all that is left. You have made it through the longest single-state stretch of Route 66, so stop for a few minutes in Texola and imagine what life was like in these little towns before crossing into the Texas panhandle.

ABOVE: *The classic Oklahoma Route 66 Museum in Clinton.*
BOTTOM: *John Carradine and Henry Fonda in John Ford's classic "The Grapes of Wrath."*
OPPOSITE: *This soothing pastoral landscape typifies the scenery around the Wichita Mountains National Refuge.*

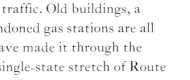

ON AND AROUND ROUTE 66: OKLAHOMA

CLAREMORE

Will Rogers Memorial Museum
1720 W. Will Rogers Blvd.
918.341.0719, www.willrogers.org
Exhibits highlight the life of Will Rogers and the works of many other notable western artists.

J. M. Davis Arms & Historical Museum
333 Lynn Riggs Blvd.
918.341.5707, www.state.ok.us/~jmdavis
One of the largest collections of arms in the world

TULSA

Gilcrease Museum
1400 Gilcrease Museum Road
918.596.2700, www.gilcrease.org
American western art featuring the works of Moran, Remington, and Russell

Big Splash Water Park
4707 E. 21st Street
918.749.7385, www.bigsplashwaterpark.com
This water theme park offers a day of wet and wild fun.

Tulsa Zoo and Living Museum
5701 E. 36th Street North
918. 669.6200, www.tulsazoo.org
See the new penguin exhibit at this world class zoo and living museum

OKLAHOMA CITY

National Cowboy and Western Heritage Museum
1700 NE 63rd Street
405.478.2250, www.nationalcowboymuseum.org
A living memorial to the men and women who settled the West

Myriad Botanical Gardens and Crystal Bridge
301 W. Reno
405.297.3995, www.myriadbotanicalgardens.com
A 224-foot long, seven-story glass cylinder that features a full botanical garden, elevated walkways, and a beautiful 35-foot waterfall

National Softball Hall of Fame and Museum
2801 NE 50th Street
405.424.5266, www.softball.org/hall_of_fame
To be in the National Softball Hall of Fame is the ultimate goal for players, coaches, and umpires, who aspire to greatness in the sport.

Oklahoma City National Memorial
620 N. Harvey
405.235.3313, www.oklahomacitynationalmemorial.org
This memorial is located at the site of the former Murrah Federal Building, which was truck-bombed in 1995.

CLINTON

Oklahoma Route 66 Museum
2229 W. Gary Freeway
580.323.7866, www.route66.org
Exhibits feature artifacts and documents from the former Highway 66 in Oklahoma. It is also the first state-sponsored Route 66 Museum in the country.

ELK CITY

Elk City Museum Complex & National Route 66 Museum
2717 3rd Street
580.225.6266, www.elkcitychamber.com/route66.asp
This complex of buildings representing pioneer life is home to the Beutler Rodeo Hall, the Farm and Ranch Museum, and the 42,000-square foot National Route 66 Museum.

TEXAS

THE LONE STAR STATE

OPPOSITE: *Sunrise welcomes Route 66 roadies to Texas as it rises over Lake Meredith National Recreation Area.* **TOP:** *Cows graze at the famous Cadillac Ranch in Amarillo.* **ABOVE:** *This wall mural celebrates Route 66 along Amarillo's 6th Street.*

TEXAS OFFERS US COWBOYS, beef on the hoof, ten Cadillacs buried nose first in the sand, a leaning water tower, one of the largest crosses in the western hemisphere, a museum devoted to barbed wire, and a free 72-ounce steak! What in the world are we waiting for—let's go visit Texas!

Shamrock is our first Texas town and there, on the right, is the U-Drop Inn, recently purchased and renovated by the city. The U-Drop Inn was built in 1936 in a classic art deco style and was considered to be "the swankiest of the swank eating places" between Oklahoma City and Amarillo.

Just ahead, McLean is home to the Devil's Rope and Route 66 Museums, which are both housed in what was once a brassiere factory. For those unfamiliar with the term, devil's rope is another name for barbed wire, and you will be amazed at the number of varieties that have been made over the years. The Route

66 portion of the museum has many excellent displays and a wonderful collection of Route 66 memorabilia, making it a must see for the traveling roadie.

Down the hill and across the plains in Groom, you will see a huge cross. This is one of the tallest crosses in the western hemisphere at 190 feet. The cross is Steve Thomas' personal statement of faith. The owner of an engineering company, Thomas had the cross erected at his own expense, and it is now administered by Cross Ministries.

THE HISTORY OF DEVIL'S ROPE

As the Great West opened for settlement, new arrivals were hard pressed for a way to fence off property and keep livestock from wandering. In the high plains of Texas, a herd would move with the wind, and in virtually no time at all, they could travel tens of miles away from the ranch. Not accustomed to the lack of wood and rock, the new landowners were perplexed at how to pen in their herds.

Smooth wire dates back to A.D. 400, and by 1870, it was readily available but impractical for use. Cattle would lean against the smooth wire and the posts would collapse under their hefty weight.

The first barbed wire design was invented by Michael Kelly in 1868, but it wasn't until 1874, when Joseph Glidden, a farmer from De Kalb, IL, perfected the wire. Glidden's wire consisted of a simple wire barb locked onto a double strand of smooth wire. The success of the Glidden wire was due not only to the simplicity of the design, but also to the fact that his invention was plain enough that it could be mass-produced. Others soon followed suit, and more than 570 patents were submitted for barbed wire. A three-year legal battle ensued, but when the courts were through with the case, the Glidden patent won, and his invention earned him the title of the Father of Barbed Wire.

Soon, barbed wire was found all over the West. Homesteaders and ranchers fenced off thousands of acres of property, and controversy arose. Religious groups protested the use of the wire, claiming the injury to livestock was "the work of the devil." Long-time inhabitants of the open plains coined the term "devil's rope," when the wire suddenly barred their passage. But the controversy was short-lived as the last of the open range was fenced off by the big cattle ranches.

Today, collectors actively search for examples of the 2,000 plus early variations of barbed wire. One of the best places to learn more about barbed wire and its fascinating history is at the Devil's Rope Museum in McLean, TX.

Also in Groom is the leaning water tower. Built by Ralph Britten in the early 1950s, it was the icon of the Britten U.S.A. Truck Stop and designed to lure interested tourists in from the highway. The truck stop is gone, but the questions and the tower remain.

Amarillo is the largest city in the Texas Panhandle and the location of more than one Route 66 attraction. Amarillo (for those of you who remember your high school Spanish, it should be *Ahm-a-ree-o*, but in Texan, it comes out as *Am-a-rill-o*) dates back to the late 1800s with a colorful past, covering everything from the sale of buffalo hides and bones, to cattle, oil, and helium. The city can even claim that it was once the primary source of the world's helium supply.

OPPOSITE: *The 192-foot-tall Cross of the Plains in Groom towers above everything for miles around.* **ABOVE:** *The U-Drop-Inn, a deco classic in Shamrock, has been restored and opened as a museum and visitor center.* **LEFT:** *The Leaning Tower of Texas at Groom still puzzles tourists at its odd construction.*

A local icon is the Big Texan Steak Ranch, where you can get a free 72-ounce steak. The catch? You have to eat it and all the trimmings in an hour. One local gourmand has done it over twenty times, but be forewarned, it ain't as easy as it looks!

Just west of Amarillo is the Cadillac Ranch, the brainchild of Stanley Marsh 3 (yep, "3"), a local rancher, farmer, and art collector. The Cadillac Ranch, with the noses of its ten vintage Cadillacs buried deeply in the sand, pays homage to the great finned beasts of the 1940s, 1950s, and 1960s.

TOP: *The Bug Ranch in Conway is a humorous imitation of the Cadillac Ranch in Amarillo.* **RIGHT AND OPPOSITE:** *Everything, including the advertising, is big at the Big Texan Steak Ranch in Amarillo.* **BOTTOM:** *Stanley Marsh 3's homage to the tail fin, Cadillac Ranch, Amarillo.*

Small towns—Bushland, Wildorado, Vega—a blink and they are gone. These tiny towns are the geographic heart of Route 66. Just past this point, the towns of Landergin and Adrian lead to the Texas-New Mexico state line at Glenrio.

Now a ghost town, Glenrio was once a thriving Route 66 community. A wide four-lane stretch of the Mother Road went straight through the center of town. Businesses, like the famous First In Texas/Last In Texas Motel and Longhorn Café did a booming business twenty-four hours a day. When the blowing snow and howling winds of a Blue Norther (a severe, cold storm from the north) whipped across the high plains, cars by the hundreds would pull into Glenrio, and the people would huddle over hot cups of coffee and swap stories about the ice up towards Amarillo or the deep drifts back towards Tucumcari. Glenrio was a sanctuary, a place to get in out of the weather and enjoy the small town atmosphere.

Today, almost all life has disappeared from Glenrio. The quietness is eerie, and the only sounds heard are the trucks on the distant interstate. Before venturing into New Mexico, be sure to stop and take some pictures of this ghost town—it might not be here in a few more years.

TOP LEFT: *Burma Shave products are still available at shops along Route 66.* **ABOVE:** *The center of Glenrio, once a bustling town but now a ghost town, offers a view of the First in Texas/Last in Texas Motel.* **BOTTOM:** *With the elimination of the Santa Fe Loop, Adrian became the mid-point of Route 66.* **OPPOSITE:** *Route 66 travelers should take a break from driving and see the grandeur of Palo Duro Canyon south of Amarillo.*

ON AND AROUND ROUTE 66: TEXAS

MCLEAN
Devil's Rope Museum
100 W. Kingsley Street
806.779.2225,
www.barbwiremuseum.com
Exhibits trace the history of barbed wire, its artifacts, the significance of the invention, and the impact on the development of the Old West. A separate section is devoted to the history of Route 66 across Texas.

AMARILLO
American Quarter Horse Heritage Center & Museum
2601 I-40 East
806.376.5181,
www.aqha.com/foundation/museum/
Chronologically arranged exhibits examine the development of the American Quarter Horse from colonial racing days to the present.

Palo Duro Canyon State Park
11450 Park Road 5
806.488.2227,
www.palodurocanyon.com
16 miles of scenic drives along "the Grand Canyon of Texas"

Cadillac Ranch
West of Amarillo between Hope and Arnott Road
This ranch pays homage to the American Dream with ten Cadillacs buried in the Texas sand.

NEW MEXICO

LAND OF ENCHANTMENT

THE MOTHER ROAD crosses the Land Of Enchantment and introduces the traveler to not only varied cultures, but also the wonders of a state where neon signs are lovingly preserved, ancient pueblos are still occupied, and a modern city proudly displays its regal heritage.

From the state line at Glenrio, Route 66 stretches across the Llano Estacado (*yawno es-tah-caw-doh*), an area that was once so treacherous and feared that early explorers would travel hundreds of miles to avoid it. The plains were dry, windswept, and unforgiving. But today, traffic doesn't slow across this region, and only those who visit the rest area near Glenrio and pause long enough to read the informative signs will understand how foreboding the Llano Estacado once was.

Past Bard, Endee, and San Jon (*san hone*), the road skirts the hills and arroyos to Tucumcari. What a wonder this town is. "Tucumcari Tonight—2,000 Motel Rooms," the signs used to proclaim all the way from Oklahoma City to Winslow, Arizona. The town, once said to be "two blocks wide and five miles long," was the place to stop for a room, a good meal, and a chance to take a break from the road.

Today, Tucumcari still thrives, although the steady stream of Route 66 traffic has long since ceased. It has become a retirement haven, beckoning the retiree with low home prices, good weather, and a laid back atmosphere free of the problems of big cities. But the classic motels are still here with the Blue Swallow, lovingly restored over the past few years, topping the list. In the early evening as the sun sets and the neon signs begin to glow, there is an honest feeling that Tucumcari still resides in the glory days of Route 66.

OPPOSITE: The beautiful Pecos River gently crosses Route 66 in Santa Rosa. **TOP:** *Lonely remains of the original alignment of Route 66 east of Santa Rosa.* **ABOVE LEFT:** *Highly-collectible antique maps of Route 66 are now quite valuable.* **ABOVE RIGHT:** *A classic motel of the Mother Road, The Blue Swallow in Tucumcari welcomes guest with its recognizable neon sign.*

Following the Route out of town, you'll pass through numerous towns—Montoya, Newkirk, and Cuervo—each now a ghost town and quietly inviting exploration. What was here? What were the people like? Where did they go?

The road finally comes down from the Llano Estacado and winds towards Santa Rosa, where you'll find more classic motels and more places serving "real" food like the Silver Moon Restaurant and The Comet II. Sadly, the once popular Club Cafe is no more. Opened in 1935, the Club Cafe was an institution, an icon of the highway, and its Fat Man logo signs were known around the world. In 1965, with the adoption of Lady Bird Johnson's Highway Beautification Act, Club Cafe owner Ron Chavez told the U.S. House of Representatives that if the small businesses could no longer

have their billboards along the interstate, it would kill them. He warned of the day when fast food franchises would come to Santa Rosa and destroy the local flavor of the community. In 1992, facing virtual bankruptcy, Ron Chavez closed Club Cafe—the same year the first fast food franchise opened in Santa Rosa. Fortunately, the famed Fat Man wasn't lost in this sad tale. He found a new home at Joseph's Restaurant in Santa Rosa.

CLUB CAFE — **ORIGINAL**
ROUTE 66
SANTA ROSA, NM — **SINCE 1935**
Two Million Sourdough Biscuits

TOP: *The Route 66 Auto Museum in Santa Rosa is a must-see attraction for any classic car fanatic.*
LEFT: *The Club Cafe was a Route 66 treasure between 1935 and 1992, but now it is only a memory.*
BOTTOM: *Once Tucumcari had over 2,000 motel rooms, but today, it still takes pride in having over 1,200 rooms for the traveling roadie.*

TUCUMCARI TONITE.
The Heart of Route 66
1200 Rooms • Only 1 Hour

TOP: *Local artists display their wares at the historic Plaza in Santa Fe.* **BOTTOM:** *Close to the Palace of the Governors is the Museum of Fine Arts in Santa Fe.*

West of Santa Rosa, Route 66 splits. In the early years of the road, it was decided that Route 66 should go through the state capital in Santa Fe and a rough road was cut through. But a hotly contested political battle in the 1930s resulted in the governor not being backed by the powers in Santa Fe, so the governor decided to take away the road. Working feverishly, the road department, knowing they would be replaced by the incoming administration, cut a new alignment through to Albuquerque in record time, taking the new path of Route 66 through Albuquerque instead of Santa Fe. Today, you can fortunately choose your route, whether you follow the direct route to Albuquerque and the city of lights or the old, pre-1937 road to Santa Fe through some of the prettiest countryside in New Mexico.

Taking the old route from Santa Rosa to Santa Fe, you'll travel the rough road as it shoots almost straight as an arrow across the high, grass-covered plains of Dilia, Los Montoyas, and Romeroville. Here the road curves left and takes you through the small towns of Tecolote, Bernal, San Jose, Pecos, and a finally over Glorieta Pass, where you cross the highest point on the original road at 7,525 feet.

Once over the pass, follow the original route down the canyon and into Santa Fe. The capital of New Mexico, Santa Fe lives up to its nickname, "The City Different." This is one of the most charming cities on old Route 66 and dates back to 1609 when it received the name La Villa Real de Santa Fe de San Francisco (The Royal City of the Holy Faith of Saint Francis). Santa Fe is an alluring city—the soft, earthen hued beauty of adobe is everywhere. A leisurely walk across the plaza slows the heart and warms the soul. Once caught up in the town's magic, you will find that the abundant art galleries, world-class hotels, and unforgettable dining make Santa Fe well worth a longer stay.

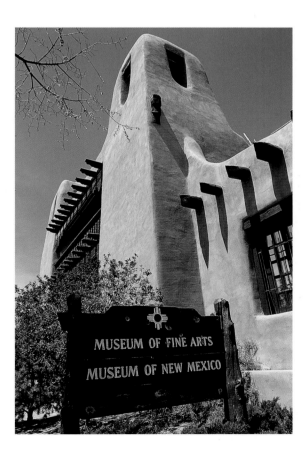

MUSEUM OF FINE ARTS
MUSEUM OF NEW MEXICO

THE GIFT SHOP WITH A ZIP CODE

On the high plains of eastern New Mexico is Cline's Corners, another testament to the perseverance of a Route 66 business-man. In 1933, Roy Cline, Sr. bought the land at the intersection of New Mexico Highways 2 and 6. With the help of his son, they built a gas station. Roy's goal was to create enough of a business that its name would land on the state map, so he asked Roy, Jr. for help with the name. Roy, Jr. studied the question for a moment and replied, "Cline's Corners."

Business was good until 1937, when the highway department moved Highway 6 north and combined it with the realign-ment of Route 66. Roy, Sr. wasn't about to let his business get away that easily, so they jacked up the building and moved it to a new location at the junction of Route 66 and New Mexico Highway 2. A few years later, Highway 2 was moved about three-quarters of a mile to the east and renumbered Highway 285. Again the building was jacked up, wheels slipped underneath, and the whole thing moved to its new location.

About this time, one of Roy's daughters married a carpenter, and Roy immediately put him to work building an addition to the service station, which was shortly followed by a café and a gift shop. By 1945, Cline's Corners was big enough to open its own postal facility for ranchers living in the area. And in 1961, when the U.S. was handing out zip codes to help organize national mail service, Cline's Corners applied and was given its very own zip code.

Cline's Corners is a true survivor. When I-40 crossed northern New Mexico, Cline's was right there at the junction of Highway 285, requiring an off-ramp to be built in order to keep the business alive. Today, Cline's Corners is a large operation with a huge gift shop, gas sta-tion, and cafeteria. One might even call it a small town. And when the winter wind blows snow across the interstate and the road turns slick and treacherous, the traveler knows that Cline's is a safe haven with hot coffee and a warm atmosphere to wait out the storm.

Oh, about that zip code, it's 87070.

Heading south from Santa Fe, it is neces-sary to take I-25 to Albuquerque in order to rejoin the more modern alignment of Route 66. As you drop off the escarpment into the Rio Grande Valley, the old highway, originally built by the Army in the 1860s and no longer usable, is off to the right. This section of road was called La Bajada Hill, a precarious eight hundred foot drop with mind-numbing 28% grades (for comparison, 7% is considered steep on today's highways). By the time Route 66 crossed La Bajada in 1926, the roadway had been improved to the point of having 23 very tight switchbacks and grades of no more than 9%. A sign at the top warned, "This road is not foolproof, but safe for a sane driver."

If you decide to take the direct, post-1937 road from Santa Rosa to Albuquerque, you will pass through Clines Corners, Longhorn Ranch, Moriarty, Edgewood, and Tijeras (Tea-harris). The cut through the hard rock of Tijeras Canyon leading into Albuquerque was a major feat of road construction.

OPPOSITE: *In October of each year the sky above Albuquerque is filled with the beauty of hot air balloons during the International Balloon Festival.* **ABOVE:** *The lovely plaza in Albuquerque's Old Town.* **RIGHT:** *A new addition to the Mother Road is the Route 66 Casino at Laguna Pueblo, a few miles west of Albuquerque.*

Setting off over a thousand charges of dyna-mite simultaneously removed such a small amount of rock that the resulting clean-up took less than twenty minutes. Nevertheless, the pass was completed, and finally, you reach Albuquerque.

Albuquerque is known as "the Duke City" and was named, in 1709, San Francisco de Alburquerque (yes, that first "r" belongs there). It was named for Francisco Xavier and the Duke of Alburquerque, Viceroy of Spain. As to that first r? Somewhere along the line, someone thought that the spelling would be easier without it, and the letter was dropped. The current (and oh so much easier) spelling of Albuquerque came into being.

LEFT: *The Route 66 Diner offers road food classics on Central Avenue in Albuquerque.* **BOTTOM LEFT:** *A neon restoration project by the New Mexico Route 66 Association has brought this dying art back to life. Now, business signs light up the sky again in true Route-66 fashion.* **BOTTOM RIGHT:** *The Court Cafe on Albuquerque's Central Avenue fed three generations of roadies with the delicious food offered on this menu.* **OPPOSITE:** *The beautiful Church of San Felipe de Neri, built in 1706, stands on the north side of Old Town Plaza in Albuquerque.*

Central Avenue through Albuquerque is a marvel for the roadies of the world. Many of the classic motels still have their wonderful signs—the art deco of Nob Hill should not be missed, and even the eclectic look of the University area can be appreciated. Old Town is another "must see" with its sidewalk merchants and handsome old church. Other classic landmarks are the Aztec Motel, the Route 66 Diner, the KiMo Theater, the El Don Motel, and the El Vado Motel. A stop at any of these Route 66 icons will offer you endless tales of the open road.

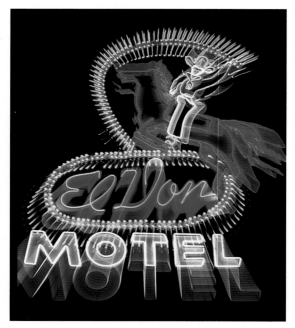

Leaving Albuquerque, the highway enters and crosses reservation lands. Please be respectful of the people who live here. Towns along the way are Laguna Pueblo, New Laguna, Paraje, Budville, Villa de Cubero—where it is said that the prolific Ernest Hemingway worked on his novel *The Old Man and the Sea*—San Fidel, McCarty's, Grants, Bluewater, The Continental Divide, Coolidge, and Gallup.

Gallup is another wonder of Route 66. Cultures do not clash here—they mingle. The Navajo, the Hopi, the Latino, and the Anglo communities work together to make Gallup a center of cultural diversity. Again, classic motels, mom and pop cafés, and amazing tourist shops combine to make Gallup an intriguing city. Some of the finest Indian jewelry in the area can be found downtown at Richardson's Trading Post, and for a unique dining experience try The Dine Grill, which specializes in Navajo cuisine. Gallup is also home to the Eagle Café, the oldest restaurant on New Mexico's Route 66, as well as classic eating establishments like Earl's Restaurant, the Ranch Kitchen, and

Virgie's Restaurant. Finally, be sure to visit El Rancho Hotel, wonderfully restored to its 1930s splendor when it was home to the stars during Gallup's Hollywood debut.

Once you leave Gallup, there are less than twenty miles to the New Mexico—Arizona state line. Amazingly, Route 66 continues to bring awe and wonder at virtually every turn.

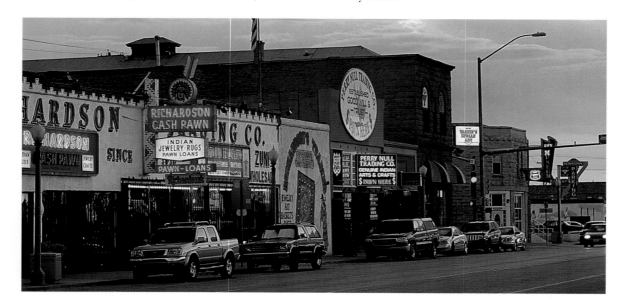

TOP: *Laguna Pueblo is shown here with the handsome San Jose de Laguna Church, built in 1699, on the top of the hill.* **ABOVE:** *The elegant lobby of the beautifully restored El Rancho Hotel in Gallup.* **LEFT:** *Lights chase away the darkness as evening descends on downtown Gallup.* **OPPOSITE:** *Wind-carved rocks typify the Cave Creek landscape near Laguna.*

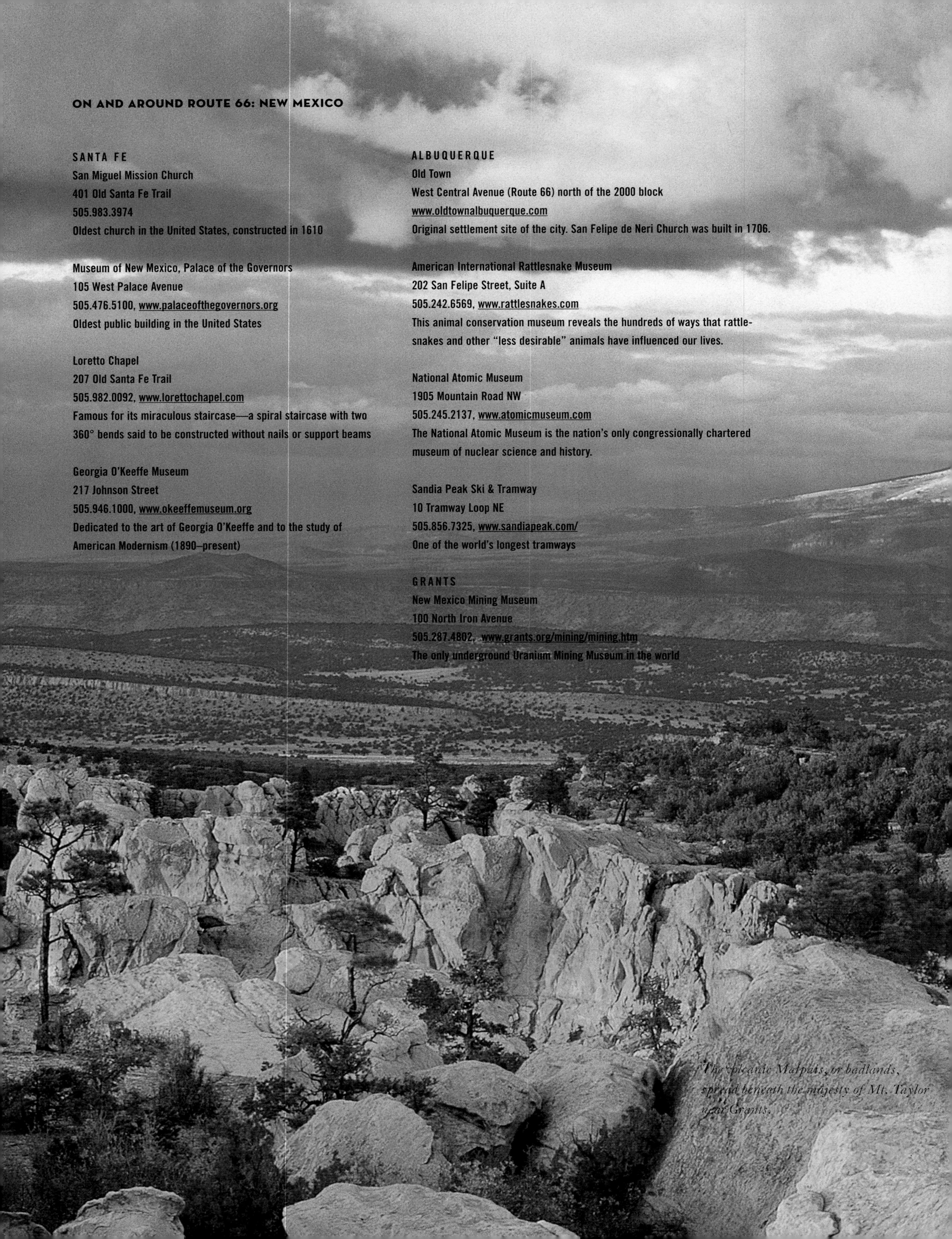

ON AND AROUND ROUTE 66: NEW MEXICO

SANTA FE

San Miguel Mission Church
401 Old Santa Fe Trail
505.983.3974
Oldest church in the United States, constructed in 1610

Museum of New Mexico, Palace of the Governors
105 West Palace Avenue
505.476.5100, www.palaceofthegovernors.org
Oldest public building in the United States

Loretto Chapel
207 Old Santa Fe Trail
505.982.0092, www.lorettochapel.com
Famous for its miraculous staircase—a spiral staircase with two
360° bends said to be constructed without nails or support beams

Georgia O'Keeffe Museum
217 Johnson Street
505.946.1000, www.okeeffemuseum.org
Dedicated to the art of Georgia O'Keeffe and to the study of
American Modernism (1890–present)

ALBUQUERQUE

Old Town
West Central Avenue (Route 66) north of the 2000 block
www.oldtownalbuquerque.com
Original settlement site of the city. San Felipe de Neri Church was built in 1706.

American International Rattlesnake Museum
202 San Felipe Street, Suite A
505.242.6569, www.rattlesnakes.com
This animal conservation museum reveals the hundreds of ways that rattle-
snakes and other "less desirable" animals have influenced our lives.

National Atomic Museum
1905 Mountain Road NW
505.245.2137, www.atomicmuseum.com
The National Atomic Museum is the nation's only congressionally chartered
museum of nuclear science and history.

Sandia Peak Ski & Tramway
10 Tramway Loop NE
505.856.7325, www.sandiapeak.com/
One of the world's longest tramways

GRANTS

New Mexico Mining Museum
100 North Iron Avenue
505.287.4802, www.grants.org/mining/mining.htm
The only underground Uranium Mining Museum in the world

The volcanic Malpais, or badlands,
spread beneath the majesty of Mt. Taylor
near Grants.

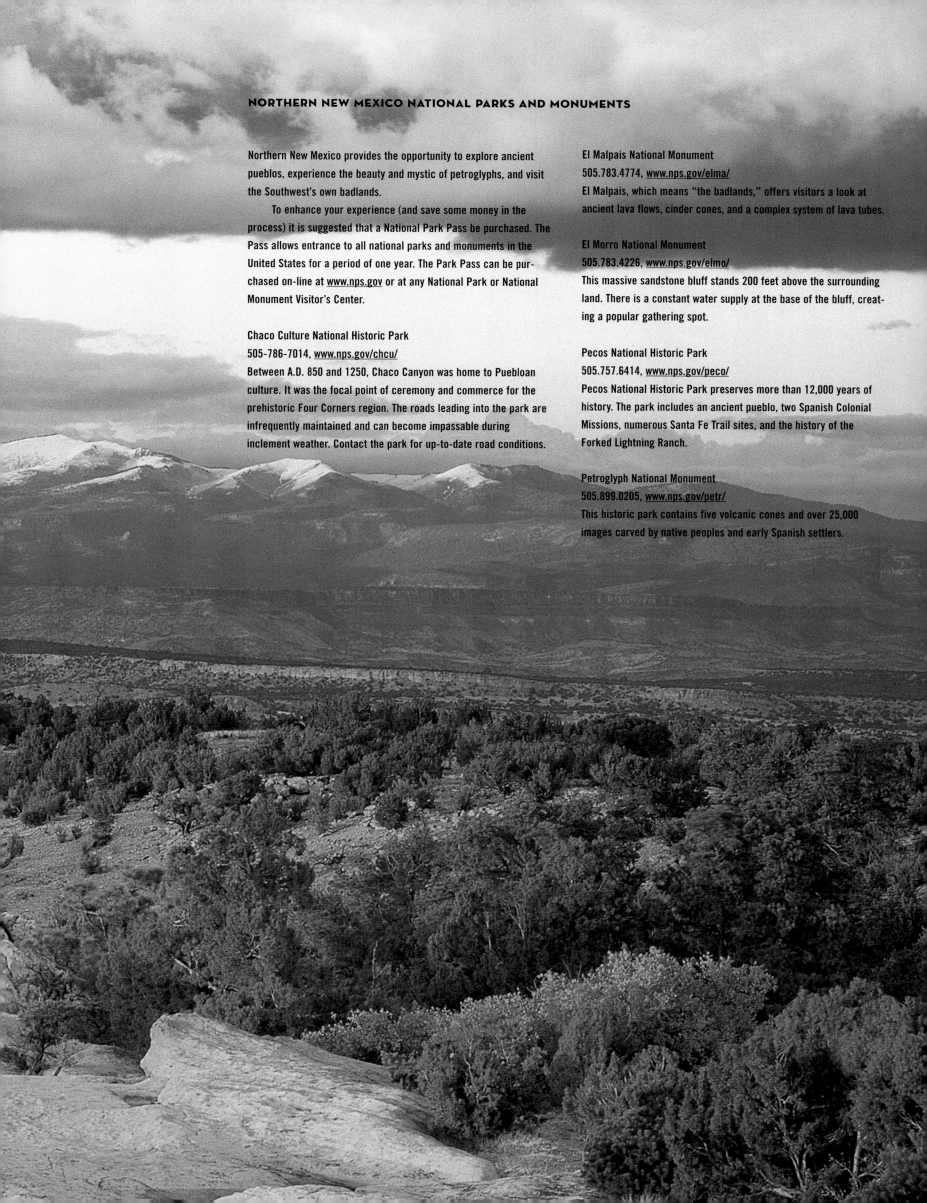

NORTHERN NEW MEXICO NATIONAL PARKS AND MONUMENTS

Northern New Mexico provides the opportunity to explore ancient pueblos, experience the beauty and mystic of petroglyphs, and visit the Southwest's own badlands.

To enhance your experience (and save some money in the process) it is suggested that a National Park Pass be purchased. The Pass allows entrance to all national parks and monuments in the United States for a period of one year. The Park Pass can be purchased on-line at www.nps.gov or at any National Park or National Monument Visitor's Center.

Chaco Culture National Historic Park
505-786-7014, www.nps.gov/chcu/
Between A.D. 850 and 1250, Chaco Canyon was home to Puebloan culture. It was the focal point of ceremony and commerce for the prehistoric Four Corners region. The roads leading into the park are infrequently maintained and can become impassable during inclement weather. Contact the park for up-to-date road conditions.

El Malpais National Monument
505.783.4774, www.nps.gov/elma/
El Malpais, which means "the badlands," offers visitors a look at ancient lava flows, cinder cones, and a complex system of lava tubes.

El Morro National Monument
505.783.4226, www.nps.gov/elmo/
This massive sandstone bluff stands 200 feet above the surrounding land. There is a constant water supply at the base of the bluff, creating a popular gathering spot.

Pecos National Historic Park
505.757.6414, www.nps.gov/peco/
Pecos National Historic Park preserves more than 12,000 years of history. The park includes an ancient pueblo, two Spanish Colonial Missions, numerous Santa Fe Trail sites, and the history of the Forked Lightning Ranch.

Petroglyph National Monument
505.899.0205, www.nps.gov/petr/
This historic park contains five volcanic cones and over 25,000 images carved by native peoples and early Spanish settlers.

ARIZONA

THE GRAND CANYON STATE

EXPERIENCE THE high desert, the smell of a pine forest, a ride on the giant jackrabbit, the amazing Grand Canyon, and the wonder of the crisp blue Colorado River as you follow Route 66 across northern Arizona. Soaring red cliffs welcome you to the Grand Canyon State. Entering Arizona from the East also places Route 66 travelers in the Navajo Nation, the largest reservation in the U.S.

The Petrified Forest National Park offers visitors a chance to examine the petrified remains of trees millions of years old. The logs in the Petrified Forest were washed into what was once a low-lying swamp, and as volcanoes to the west spewed tons of ash into the area, the logs were buried in the sediment. Water passing over the buried logs caused the silica in the ash to dissolve into the logs, which replaced the cell walls and crystallized into mineral quartz. Minerals rich in iron combined with the quartz to produce the brilliant colors. That's the accepted story of the Petrified Forest—now for the local Indian legend. A goddess was tired and hungry. When she discovered the logs lying on the ground, she killed a rabbit and attempted to light a fire. The logs were soaked and would not ignite. In her anger she turned the logs to stone.

It is illegal to remove any of the petrified wood from the area. Souvenirs may be purchased in the park gift shop or at various trading posts along the highway. These petrified pieces of wood are harvested from areas outside the park boundaries.

OPPOSITE: *Petrified logs cascade down a canyon at Blue Mesa in the Petrified Forest National Park.*
TOP: *The old highway between Kingman and Oatman provides a serious climb for one of the participants during the annual Arizona Route 66 Association Fun Run.*
BOTTOM: *A shop owner inspects petrified wood, gathered legally from outside of the park's boundaries, before sealing the deal.*

TOP: *The Painted Desert offers fantastic colors brought about by the change of seasons, or even the time of day.*
BOTTOM LEFT: *Commodore Perry Owens, Sheriff of Apache County, poses with his trusty rifle in 1887.*
BOTTOM RIGHT: *Roadside attractions that offer outstanding views of petrified logs and fossils dominate the scene just east of Holbrook.*

Before leaving the park, be sure to take in the spectacular views of the Painted Desert, an area where colors change depending on the time of day or season of the year.

Holbrook, 25 miles west of the park's main entrance, was once known as the "town too tough for churches," since it was the only county seat in the nation without a church. With the coming of the railroad in 1881, the town became an important shipping point for cattle, wool, and hides, and with the cattle came the cowboys. With money in their pockets and saloons on every corner, Holbrook was known for barroom brawls and street fights. September of 1887 saw one of the West's most

spectacular gunfights: the Graham-Tewksbury feud (also known as the Pleasant Valley war). On September 2, Andy Blevins, a cattle rustler from Texas, rode into Holbrook after a shootout in Pleasant Valley, where he had killed two men. Apache County sheriff, C. P. Owens, rode into town with a cattle-rustling warrant for Blevins. He went to the Blevins' home, and within minutes, Andy, his brother Sam, and another relative were dead and John Blevins was wounded.

Today, Holbrook is a quiet community, complete with churches and motels, such as the famous Wigwam Motel. Built in 1950 by Chester Lewis, the Wigwam Motel is a testament to the perseverance of the Route 66

RIGHT: *The beautiful La Posada, a former Harvey House, has been restored to its former glory in Winslow.*
BELOW: *"Here It Is!" beckons the Jackrabbit, which still offers wonderful Route 66 souvenirs and a chance to have your picture taken on the back of a giant jackrabbit.* **BOTTOM:** *The Wigwam Motel in Holbrook offers travelers a very unique place to spend the night.*

business owner. Chester operated the motel until 1974, closing it when the interstate diverted business away from Holbrook. In 1988, Chester's son, John Lewis, began the huge task of restoring the Wigwam. Finally remodeled and reopened, the Wigwam Motel once again provides thousands of visitors the chance to "Sleep in a Wigwam."

"Here It Is!" the billboard all but shouts. For hundred of miles in either direction the small jackrabbit signs sit alongside Route 66, promising...? Kids in the backseat wonder what amazing sights await,

and they pleadingly ask to stop once they reach the huge billboard. The Jackrabbit is a tourist stop that opened in 1947 and has been a steady icon of the road ever since. Be sure to have your picture taken atop the giant jackrabbit and try a cup of their one-of-a-kind cherry cider.

Winslow, a once booming railroad town, is home to the classic La Posada, a former Harvey House designed by famed architect Mary Jane Colter. Beautifully restored in the 1990s, La Posada once again offers classic rooms and world-class dining. While in town, be sure to stop by the Standin' on the Corner Park and have your picture taken Standin' on a Corner in Winslow, Arizona.

The park was created to pay homage to The Eagles 1972 hit song, "Take it Easy." When planning out the contents of the park, the committee decided that if it wasn't in the song, it wouldn't be in the park. Artists and sculptors were contacted and the vision started coming to life. A two-story mural by Trope L'oeil artist John Pugh was painted on the building at the back of the park, a life-size bronze statue of a man "standing on a corner" by Ron Adamson was appropriately placed on the corner, and finally, bricks inscribed with personalized messages were set into the sidewalk. On September 10, 1999, the Standin' on the Corner Park was dedicated and now receives hundreds of visitors each year.

Meteor Crater was created approximately 50,000 years ago when a meteorite 150 feet across, weighing 300,000 tons, and traveling at 40,000 miles an hour collided with the earth's surface. With an airblast in excess of 1,200 miles an hour, virtually every living thing within fifteen miles of the impact site was scoured from the earth.

Continuing west, the land changes dramatically from grasslands to scrub juniper. Soon you cross Canyon Padre and arrive at Twin Arrows. Originally established as the Canyon Padre Trading Post, Twin Arrows became a Route 66 landmark with the construction of a pair of leaning telephone poles with plywood feathers attached. Owned by

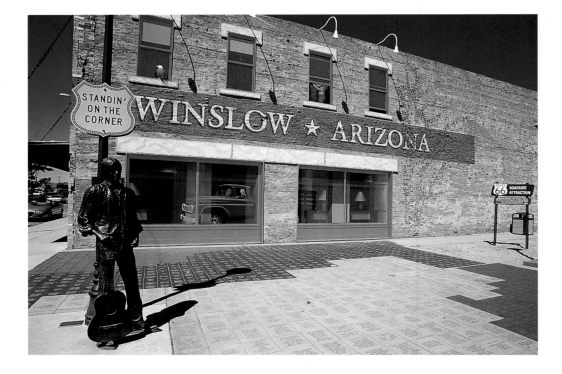

the Troxell family of Flagstaff, Twin Arrows served the motoring public with a gas station, a delightful diner, a general store, and, of course, a gift shop. When I-40 by-passed this stretch of Route 66, Twin Arrows cycled through numerous owners, none of whom could bring in a profit. Finally, in 1998, Twin Arrows closed and the land reverted back to the Arizona State Land Trust. Even though this historic stop is now closed, you can still see the sturdy twin arrows standing watch over the approaching ponderosa pine forest.

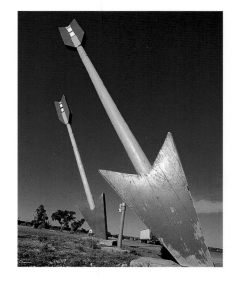

TOP: *The Standin' on the Corner Park in Winslow salutes the Eagles hit "Take It Easy" with a great mural depicting the song's lyrics.* **ABOVE:** *The twin arrows still stand tall even though the gas station and diner have long been closed.* **LEFT:** *Sunset Crater northeast of Flagstaff offers a chance to explore a dormant volcano and a series of ice caves.* **OPPOSITE:** *The intricate designs of Navajo rugs and the exquisite carvings of Hopi Kachinas make southwestern Native American art highly valued by collectors throughout the world.*

BUYING NATIVE AMERICAN ARTS AND CRAFTS

By Kathleen Bryant

Travel the Southwest, and you'll discover an astonishing variety of Indian arts and crafts, from delicate Zuni fetishes to room-sized Navajo rugs. Whether you're a serious collector or simply want to buy something special to remember your journey, you can educate yourself by attending shows and festivals and by talking with sales personnel and artists.

Many artists learned their skills from a grandmother, uncle, or other family member, and traditions reach back through generations— sometimes even centuries. Modern tools and materials have inspired exquisite craftsmanship and experimentation, though handwork is still the hallmark of Native American art.

Hopi jeweler Duane Tawahongva, for example, handcrafts everything in his jewelry, even the tiny bails and links in his silver overlay pieces. Many kachina carvers use simple tools like dremels in their work, though others—particularly carvers of traditional-style tihus (dolls)—will use only a knife and rasp. Acoma pottery, with its dazzling fine-line decoration, might be kiln-fired to eliminate fire clouds, while many Hopi potters prefer using dung fires, believing the smoky shadings make each piece unique.

Hopi potter Lawrence Namoki advises buyers to look for signs of careful craftsmanship, such as fineness of line in designs. Precise details are important to most crafts, as are pleasing proportions and symmetry. Baskets and rugs should be tightly woven, and rugs should lie flat. Prices will reflect the skill and reputation of the artist as well as his or her investment in time.

Unfortunately, the high value of Indian art has tempted unscrupulous companies to produce counterfeits. Be cautious when shopping outside established trading posts and galleries. The Indian Arts and Crafts Act of 1990 makes it illegal to market any non-Indian product as an authentic Indian-made item. If you are in doubt, you can request that vendors produce written certification that their wares are made by Indian artisans.

It is good to also be aware that not everything marked "Indian made" is handcrafted by an individual artist. Indian-owned factories and co-ops produce lovely jewelry and pottery, for example, but items are created assembly-line style, and the prices and quality usually reflect this.

After all, the wisest purchase is one you'll feel good wearing, giving, or displaying in your home. Much more than a good investment, authentic handmade Indian art is a link between you, the artist, and traditions that extend back through time.

local saddle maker, Doc Williams, bought the building and turned it into a nightclub, keeping the stuffed heads scattered throughout the building for atmosphere. Today, the good old sounds of country music fill the building, but local legend has it that the ghost of Dean Eldridge, who hated country music, still haunts the stairs and hallways.

While in Flagstaff, make sure to spend at least a day strolling through the recently renovated historic downtown. Offering a wide variety of shops and restaurants as well as an open-air central square, you'll find that Flagstaff provides all the necessities for a pleasant day on the town.

West of Flagstaff is the highest point on the post-1937 Route 66 alignment, topping off at a dizzying height of 7,335 feet. This is also the location of the Arizona Divide, so enjoy the breathtaking views!

The heart of northern Arizona can be found in Flagstaff. At approximately 7,000 feet in elevation, this is the cultural center of the region. Classic motels line the highway from east Flagstaff all the way through town. Mom and pop cafés still serve great road food—check out Miz Zip's for breakfast and La Fonda for an authentic Mexican food dinner.

The Museum Club in east Flagstaff is a classic road stop, dating back to 1931 when Dean Eldridge built what was considered to be the largest log cabin in the Southwest. As the local taxidermist, Eldridge filled his home with trophy heads of all kinds of Southwest creatures. In 1936, Eldridge passed away and a

OPPOSITE: *A meadow of wildflowers marches towards the ponderosa forest that leads up the slopes to the mighty San Francisco Peaks, the highest point in Arizona.* **TOP LEFT:** *The Hotel Monte Vista has served Flagstaff well since 1927 as the premier hotel in the downtown area.* **ABOVE:** *The Museum Club in east Flagstaff has long been a favorite for country artists visiting Northern Arizona. If you love country, you're bound to be pleased.* **BOTTOM:** *Miz Zip's on East 66 in Flagstaff has long been known as THE Breakfast place for locals and roadies alike.*

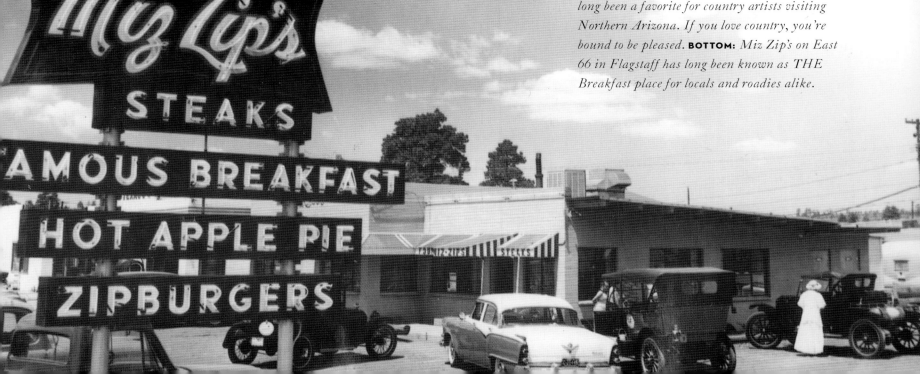

less enclosures, allowing you to interact with deer, bison, elk, reindeer, llamas, and other wildlife as well.

Williams has the distinction of being the last town on Route 66 to be by-passed by the interstate. On October 13, 1984, it became possible to drive from Chicago to Los Angeles and not encounter a single traffic light.

In order to keep business alive in Williams, the Grand Canyon Railway reestablished service from Williams to the Grand Canyon in 1989 and has since become one of the top excursion railways in the nation.

Parks is home to the Parks in the Pines General Store, a great example of a business that has been in place for nearly three-quarters of a century. This friendly general store is still serving the tiny community. West of Parks is the Garland Prairie Vista Point—an excellent place to get a memorable photo of the San Francisco Peaks.

The Deer Farm has been in business since 1969 and is a classic roadside attraction, especially for kids. Housed in what appears to be an old barn, the Deer Farm gift shop is just the tip of the iceberg. Once outside, follow the paved pathway that winds through count-

Down the hill is Ash Fork. Although seemingly deserted, this once thriving railroad town is seeing a rebirth, as retirees buy land and build new homes. Near the center of town is DeSoto's—you can't miss it; it's the place with the 1960 DeSoto on the roof. The current owners rescued an old Texaco station that had fallen into disrepair. They carefully cleaned it, remodeled everything, and opened a beauty and barbershop to serve the community.

OPPOSITE: *Every day the Grand Canyon Railway takes passengers on a trip back in time between Williams and the Grand Canyon.*

ABOVE: *Rendezvous days is celebrated each year in Williams, where mountain men join with classic cars for the parade down Route 66.*

ABOVE RIGHT: *A 1959 DeSoto with Elvis behind the wheel welcomes visitors to DeSoto's Beauty and Barber Shop in Ash Fork...a true icon of the road!*

RIGHT: *Route 66 souvenirs and a chocolate sundae from the retro-50s soda fountain make Twisters in Williams a natural stop.*

West of Ash Fork at Crookton Road is one of the longest continuous stretches of Route 66 still in use. From here to the Colorado River at Topock, there are nearly 160 miles of original Route 66.

This original stretch of road climbs and twists across the lava hills before dropping onto the large plain and entering Seligman. In 1882, Seligman was known as Prescott Junction, where the Prescott and Arizona Central Railroad met the Atlantic and Pacific Railroad (now the BNSF). The town was renamed in 1886 to honor the Seligman brothers, who were major stockholders in the Atlantic and Pacific Railroad. When Seligman was bypassed in September of 1978, it was as if someone had shut off a water tap. Local barber Angel Delgadillo watched as business dropped to almost nothing. Not being one to just let things go, he and sixteen other people from surrounding communities decided that the heritage of Route 66 was vital to our nation's history, so in 1987, the group founded the Arizona Historic Route 66 Association.

Just up the street is the Snow Cap Drive-in, operated by Angel's brother Juan. What's not to like about a place that specializes in "Cheeseburgers with Cheese" and "Dead Chicken?" You'll immediately sense there is something strange about the Snow Cap when you find two doorknobs on the main door—don't worry, you'll pick the wrong one. Inside, the atmosphere continues to perplex the first-timer, as orders are always misunderstood, small drinks are presented in cups so tiny that they're almost invisible, and a word of advice? Don't even think of asking for a small dipped cone. The Snow Cap is a living example of how good food and fun can co-exist. Oh yeah, be sure to ask for mustard with your burger.

OPPOSITE: *A gift shop in Seligman is home to one of Detroit's more famous orphans—a 1959 Edsel.* TOP: *Angel Delgadillo, former Seligman town barber and one of the founders of the Arizona Historic Route 66 Association.* ABOVE: *The Roadkill 66 Cafe in Seligman offers up good food in a western atmosphere—and, oh yeah, the roadkill is always fresh.* RIGHT: *The Snow Cap cruiser still manages to hit the road from one end of Seligman to the other.*

the dry desert air and hundreds of acres of open land made this air field the perfect location to store over 7,000 retired aircraft.

Today, Kingman is experiencing growth as the county seat for Mohave County. Be sure to stop at the Powerhouse on the west end of town, as it houses a wonderful Route 66 museum and gift shop.

Continuing west on Old 66, you'll come to the Black Mountains and what was once the most feared section of the road—the climb over Sitgreaves Pass. As the climb begins, Cool Springs Camp appears on the right. A once thriving tourist camp, café, and gas station, Cool Springs burned in 1964. It was rebuilt (kinda) in 1991 for the Jean-Claude Van Damme film "Universal Soldier," and then blown up as part of the movie. Today, the site is being lovingly restored.

The road west of Seligman crosses the great expanse of the Aubrey Valley before reaching the Grand Canyon Caverns, a tourist stop dating back to the early 1930s. Continuing on past the caverns, you'll reach Peach Springs, the tribal headquarters of the Hualapai (*wall-a-pie*) tribe. The Hualapai (People of the Tall Pines) have occupied the land around the Colorado River of north central Arizona for over 800 years.

A blink of an eye signals the passing of Truxton and Valentine before arriving at Hackberry and the Hackberry General Store. This is a great place to stop, stretch your legs, and meet John and Kerry Pritchard, who have done a wonderful job of restoring the old store building.

Beyond Antares Point, the road straightens out and shoots directly towards the heart of Kingman. Approaching the city, watch for the Kingman Airport on the left. After World War II,

OPPOSITE: *The brilliant hues of the prickly pear cactus provide color to the stark desert landscape west of Kingman.* **TOP:** *The Powerhouse Museum in Kingman features many great exhibits tracing the early days of Route 66 across Arizona.*
ABOVE: *Finding your way is never a problem on Route 66, however, getting the car started might be a little difficult. This famous scene is just outside of Truxton.* **RIGHT:** *Classic neon is a highlight of the Kingman Club in downtown Kingman.*
PAGES 60-61: *Marilyn and Elvis live in style at the Hackberry General Store's classic reproduction of a fifties-era diner.*

Farther up the hill and around the bend is Ed's Camp. Operated from the 1920s until the late 1970s, Ed's Camp and the Kactus Kafé were welcome respites from the heat. Ed's Camp has the distinction of having the only saguaro cactus on Route 66. Originally there were two, but sadly, one blew down in a windstorm in 2002. Even though Ed's has been closed for a long time now, it still attracts tourists desiring pictures of the infamous icon.

The road narrows as it twists back and forth until finally reaching the top of Sitgreaves Pass, otherwise known as Gold Hill Summit, at an elevation of 3,515 feet. Many years ago, there was an ice cream parlor located here, providing the opportunity for both car and driver to take a break and cool down after the vicious climb.

Heading down the road, you eventually enter Oatman, a picture-book mining town, complete with burros roaming the streets and staged gunfights. Carrots to feed the burros are available in local stores, giving you the opportunity to make a new friend for life—or until the carrots run out.

On the afternoon of October 1, 1952, Oatman changed forever. A ribbon was cut opening the Yucca cut-off, a new road that sent traffic south from Kingman to Topock. No longer was the climb over the Black Mountains necessary. On October 2, six of the seven gas stations in Oatman closed, and the fate of the town looked grim. As the

years passed, Oatman continued to hold on by serving the miners in the area. Then, as luck would have it, a major segment of the film "How the West Was Won" was filmed in Oatman, and the town suddenly discovered the value of being a real old West town for the traveling tourist.

As Route 66 continues south, it crosses dry desert lands, scorched by the searing sun. The retirement community of Golden Shores passes by in a rush, and then the road follows the low-lying grasses and reeds along the Colorado River. A turn under a railroad overpass, a curve up a slight hill, and there, across the interstate, is the bridge to California.

ON AND AROUND ROUTE 66: ARIZONA

FLAGSTAFF

Lowell Observatory
1400 W. Mars Hill Road
928.774.3358, www.lowell.edu
Planet Pluto was discovered here.

Museum of Northern Arizona
3101 N. Fort Valley Road
928.774.5213, www.musnaz.org
Exhibits related to Northern Arizona and the museum's four
main disciplines: anthropology, biology, geology, and fine art

The Arizona Snowbowl
Highway 180 and Snowbowl Road
928.779.1951, www.arizonasnowbowl.com
Ride the lift to the top of the mountain and ski in the winter
and take in the breathtaking views in the summer

WILLIAMS

Grand Canyon Railway
233 N. Grand Canyon Blvd.
800.THE.TRAIN, www.thetrain.com
Experience a train ride to the Grand Canyon behind a classic
steam engine.

KINGMAN

The Powerhouse Visitor Center
and Route 66 Museum
120 W. Andy Devine
928.753.9889, www.kingmantourism.org/to-do-and-see/muse-
ums/route-66-museum
A unique Route 66 museum located in the historic
powerhouse building

NORTHERN ARIZONA
NATIONAL PARKS AND MONUMENTS

Northern Arizona has more national parks and monuments
on or around Route 66 than any other state, providing the
opportunity to see the remains of ancient cultures, dormant
volcanoes, and one of the most amazing sights in the world—
the Grand Canyon.

Grand Canyon National Park
928.638.7888, http://www.nps.gov/grca/
The beauty of the Grand Canyon is unparalleled. The park, which
offers one of the most spectacular examples of erosion, is also
a World Heritage Site.

Montezuma Castle National Monument
928.567.3322, www.nps.gov/moca
Nestled into a limestone recess high above Beaver Creek
stands one of the best preserved cliff dwellings in North
America, the 600-year-old, five-story, 20-room home to the
Sinagua.

Petrified Forest National Park
928.524.6228, www.nps.gov/pefo
The 93,533-acre park features one of the world's largest and
most colorful concentrations of petrified wood. Also included
are the multi-hued badlands of the Painted Desert.

Sunset Crater Volcano National Monument
928.526.0502, www.nps.gov/sucr
Ancient inhabitants undoubtedly witnessed the eruption of this
Volcano in A.D. 1064-1065, which blanketed the region with
black cinders.

Walnut Canyon National Monument
928.526.3367, www.nps.gov/waca
The Sinagua, who lived in Walnut Canyon over 900 years ago,
built single-story dwellings under the limestone overhangs. Walk
in their footsteps and imagine how they lived.

Wupatki National Monument
928.679.2365, http://www.nps.gov/wupa/
Visit pueblos and cliff dwellings so well preserved that it's hard
to believe their builders moved on 700 years ago.

CALIFORNIA

THE GOLDEN STATE

OPPOSITE: *Wildflowers add a touch of spring color to the Kelso Dunes in the Mojave Desert.* **TOP:** *Route 66 can seem like a lonely road across the Mojave Desert.* **ABOVE:** *The water bag was once looked upon as a necessity for making that dangerous desert crossing.*

CROSSING THE COLORADO RIVER provides an air of excitement to any Route 66 trip. After more than 2,100 miles, you have finally reached the Golden State. New adventures await—the Mojave Desert, orange groves, Hollywood, and the Pacific Ocean. The road beckons and we must answer her siren call.

Ahead lies the desert, no longer as foreboding as it was during the Dust Bowl, but there is still an important common sense rule for traveling across this vast expanse of land—make certain you have plenty of water! Stop in Needles and buy a few bottles of water, not soda or beer as they will dehydrate you, but cool, clean water.

Needles was founded in 1883 with the coming of the railroad, and the railroad is still a major component of the town. Additional engines are added here for the climb across the desert to Barstow. In the center of town is the El Garces, formerly the Santa Fe Depot. Set amongst a virtual oasis of palms, palo verde, and tamarind trees, the El Garces stands as a reminder of when train travel was paramount in this country. In 1993, the city of Needles purchased the historic structure in order to preserve it, much like La Posada in Winslow.

Leaving Needles you begin to climb. The old route follows the National Old Trails Road alongside the train tracks through Goffs, a small watering station for the old steam trains. Just to the north is the old Goff's Schoolhouse. The Mojave Desert Heritage and Cultural Association has taken the schoolhouse and surrounding grounds and developed a living museum dedicated to the history of the Mojave region.

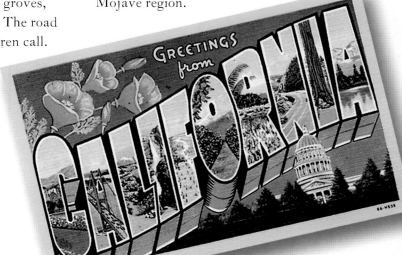

Fully staffed by volunteers, the Museum is open the first weekend of each month, except for July, August, and September and is well worth the visit.

Continuing up the old road, you'll pass through Fenner and then into Essex. This tiny town had fifteen whole minutes of fame in 1977, when it was featured on Johnny Carson's "Tonight Show" as the only town in America without a television.

Have you noticed anything about the town names yet? There were Goffs, Fenner, and Essex, and next is Danby. Originally, the locations across the Mojave were named by the railroad company in alphabetical order beginning with Amboy, and followed by Bristol, Cadiz, Danby, Essex, Fenner, Goffs, Homer, Ibis, and Java. However, with the expansion of the rail system and the addition of passing tracks, the sequence fell apart.

Past Danby is one of the most graffiti-covered buildings in the country. This location was once known as Summit, the site of a store, gas station, garage, and cabins. Nothing more than a tourist stop, Summit closed with the opening of I-40 to the north. The wooden buildings were quickly vandalized and finally removed, leaving only the stark white concrete walls of the old garage, which became a haven for the graffiti artists of the world.

Does Amboy look familiar? You have probably seen it in dozens of commercials and numerous movies. Inside the café just to the right of the cash register is where Brad Pitt, playing the psychotic Early Grace, shot-gunned the station attendant in the film "Kalifornia." Scenes from "The Hitcher" were also filmed here along with commercials for everything from cigarettes to Kit-Kat™ bars to motorcycles. At one time there were two gas stations in Amboy, one on either side of the highway. It didn't matter which one you stopped at—gas was a high 50¢ a gallon when the rest of the country was down around 19¢. That's what comes with all the fame.

ABOVE: *Michelle Forbes, Brad Pitt, Juliette Lewis, and David Duchovny take the Road Trip from hell in "Kalifornia."* **BELOW:** *Sometimes there just wasn't any more life in the old girl, so where she stopped is where she stayed. This old classic made its home in Goffs.*

KEEPING IT COOL ON THE ROAD

From the 1930s to the 1950s, no trip across the dreaded desert region of Route 66 was complete without a water bag hanging from the hood ornament of the car. Made from canvas and available at virtually every stop west of Flagstaff, the water bag was a necessity.

Desert hills, high temperatures, and a blazing sun would often take their toll on the overloaded car as it pushed its way across the Mojave. If you weren't careful, the car would overheat, sending a plume of steam into the air. Dad would grudgingly bring the car to a stop alongside the road. Other drivers would pass, glancing over with a sympathetic look that said, "I've been there, pal."

And then the wait... It was foolish to open the radiator cap right away, as the radiator would literally explode, sending a geyser of scalding water skyward. A few minutes would pass, and Dad would get anxious. "Stand back," he would order as he wrapped his hand in a rag and carefully opened the radiator cap. If he had waited long enough, there would be gurgle from deep inside and a slight whisper of steam would escape. Looking into the radiator he'd say, "Yep, she's down."

The water bag was taken from the bumper, opened, and the water, now cool from the continuous stream of air that had passed over the bag as the car sped down the road, was slowly poured into the radiator. Once the radiator was full, everyone would pile back into the car and set off once again.

"Remember to fill the water bag at the next stop," Dad would say, "It wouldn't do not to have any water out here."

Today, the water bag is a curiosity, bartered on eBay and placed on classic cars during car shows, but not so long ago, the water bag was a life-saver.

ABOVE: *The classic beauty of the Casa del Desierto Harvey House has been restored in Barstow.* **RIGHT:** *Calico Ghost Town is now a San Bernardino County Park and offers the chance to explore unique turn-of-the-century buildings and shops.*

Nine miles from Amboy in the middle of a barren spot of scraped earth is a lone tree. This was Bagdad, a long ago boomtown with hotels, churches, saloons, a school, a railroad station, and cafés. But Bagdad is no more. Legend has it that a pipeline company bull-dozed the area flat to use for storing pipe during a big construction phase in 1991...but that's not quite the way I see it. Having stopped here during a violent windstorm, I suspect the entire town was blown off to the south and now resides somewhere out on the Twenty-Nine Palms Gunnery Range.

Old maps will show the locations of Klondike and Siberia ahead—obviously some-one had a great sense of humor in naming these two locations. Klondike is gone, but there is still a shell of a building standing in Siberia.

Ludlow is another boomtown of the past. Today, it quietly tends to the needs of the tourists racing between L.A. and Laughlin. On the east side of town, the ruins of the Ludlow Café served as the main set for the film "Kalifornia."

Continuing west, the land develops into rolling hills and then settles into a long stretch of dry lakebeds. Off to the left, a large lava field from ancient eruptions in the Newberry Mountains appears to be a shadow caused by a cloud—but trust me, you won't see any clouds here.

Newberry Springs is the home of the Bagdad Café, where the movie of the same name was filmed. Director Percy Adlon came to the desert after reading about the magic that was Alice Lawrence's *Bagdad Café*, and found the original Bagdad Café long gone. He pressured the old Sidewinder Café in Newberry Springs into service, and the rest is cinematic history. Today, stills from the film decorate the walls of the Bagdad Café as legions of Europeans, who have turned the film a cult classic, are served good old road food.

The next town along the route is Barstow, the location of one of the largest intermodal operations in the country. Fully loaded trains, stretching over a mile in length, arrive in Barstow. Their cargo is quickly unloaded, and hauled off by thousands of semi-trucks to destinations all over the West. Nearby is the nicely restored Casa del Desierto, a historic Harvey House. Inside this beautiful building, you will find the Route 66 Museum.

Route 66 continues towards Victorville, but first, be prepared for a strange site: the Bottle Tree Ranch. Elmer Long has been working on this hidden treasure for about five years. Most of the bottles are old, and were found scattered across the desert. Throughout the years, Elmer constructed countless bottle "trees" and topped each one with Route 66 memorabilia such as an old sign, a 1920s typewriter, or a toy train. This unique ranch is definitely worth a visit.

At Victorville, join I-15 south and head to Cajon Pass. When Route 66 was a two-lane track down the mountain, Cajon Pass was one of those places where Mom was always shouting at Dad, "Do you HAVE to pass everything on the road?" all the while digging her fingernails deeper into the arm of the seat.

If you're a train buff, this is a great area for photographing trains. But there is one caveat—be extremely cautious near the tracks! Trains going down the steep canyon use dynamic braking, and in many cases, they cannot be heard until they are nearly on you. Enjoy, but be careful.

Cajon Pass finally opens up into what is known as the Inland Empire, the great valley covering over 200 square miles of southern California land. San Bernardino is the largest city in the Inland Empire and was named, in 1810, for the feast day of Saint San Bernardino de Siena. In 1852, a group of Mormon settlers purchased the San Bernardino ranch land from Jose de Carmen Lugo and his two brothers, paying $77,500 for the property. (Can you even imagine the current price of this prime real estate?)

In 1948, the McDonald brothers built the first McDonald's in the country in San Bernardino, introducing the nation to the concept of SpeeDee Service. In 1953, Ray Kroc, a milkshake machine salesman from Chicago, bought the franchise rights and the rest is fast food history.

"ROUTE 66"

In 1960, actors Martin Milner and George Maharis set out in a brand new Corvette to break ground with an exciting new television series about two young guys, Tod and Buz, traveling the country in search of adventures and life. "route 66" (note that the "r" is always lowercase for the TV show) was the first television series to go on location all across the country, requiring several eighteen wheelers and a crew of fifty, who were constantly creating on-the-spot techniques to make the series come alive. For four years and 116 episodes, "route 66" offered fine dramatic entertainment. In the midst of the third season, George Maharis came down with a severe case of meningitis and was forced to leave the series. He was replaced by Glen Corbett, who took the role of Linc (Lincoln) Case.

Although named for the famous highway, only two episodes were actually filmed on Route 66, one in Needles, CA, and the other along the pre-1937 route in Santa Fe, NM.

A STAR IS BORN

Route 66 typifies America's love for the open road, and the film-maker took that passion and glorified it on the big screen. From the classic "The Grapes of Wrath" to the gentle humor of "Bagdad Cafe," the iconic image of Route 66 has provided an emotional bond for people all around the world. The following is a partial list of films shot on the Mother Road, as well as the locations on the route where they were filmed:

BAGDAD CAFE, 1988, comedy/drama
C.C.H. Pounder, Jack Palance, Marianne Sägebrecht
Newberry Springs, CA

EASY RIDER, 1969, drama
Peter Fonda, Dennis Hopper
Colorado River crossing, AZ/CA; Bellemont, AZ; Flagstaff, AZ;
Santa Fe, NM

FORREST GUMP, 1994, drama/comedy
Tom Hanks, Robin Wright Penn, Sally Field, Gary Sinise
Flagstaff, AZ; Winona, AZ; Twin Arrows, AZ

THE GRAPES OF WRATH, 1940, drama
Henry Fonda, Jane Darwell, John Carradine
Route 66 from Tulsa, OK to Barstow, CA

THE HITCHER, 1986, action/horror
C. Thomas Howell, Rutger Hauer
Old Route 66 between Essex and Ludlow, CA

HOLLYWOOD OR BUST, 1956, comedy
Dean Martin, Jerry Lewis, Pat Crowley
Chain of Rocks Bridge, IL/MO; Oklahoma City, OK;
The Alvarado (Harvey House) in Albuquerque, NM

KALIFORNIA, 1993, action/drama
Brad Pitt, Juliette Lewis, David Duchovny, Michelle Forbes
Amboy, CA; Ludlow, CA

NATURAL BORN KILLERS, 1994, action/drama
Woody Harrelson, Juliette Lewis, Robert Downey, Jr.
Winslow, AZ; Gallup, NM

TWO-LANE BLACKTOP, 1971, drama
Warren Oates, James Taylor, Dennis Wilson
Needles, CA; Flagstaff, AZ; Tucumcari, NM

UNIVERSAL SOLDIER, 1992, action/science-fiction
Jean-Claude Van Damme, Dolph Lundgren
Kingman, AZ; Ash Fork, AZ

WAKING UP IN RENO, 2001, comedy/romance
Billy Bob Thornton, Patrick Swayze, Charlize Theron,
Natasha Richardson
Amarillo, TX

OPPOSITE TOP LEFT: *The Bottle Tree Ranch south of Barstow demands investigation. It's just one of the many unusual attractions along historic Route 66.*

OPPOSITE BOTTOM LEFT: *The first McDonald's is now a museum in San Bernardino, and, being on Route 66, it is a must-see for kids of all ages.*

RIGHT: *Dennis Hopper, Peter Fonda, and Jack Nicholson take to the road to discover America, and unfortunately, they find it in the 1969 film "Easy Rider."*

These and other American phenomena are celebrated each year in September at the Route 66 Rendezvous. This event draws hundreds of thousands of people to the four-day festival, all honoring the Mother Road with car shows, vendor booths, music, and constant entertainment.

From San Bernardino, Route 66 traverses the foothills of the San Gabriel Mountains, traveling past miles of orange groves. The road heads west through Rialto, Fontana, Upland, Claremont, La Verne, Glendora, and Azusa before reaching the beauty of Pasadena.

From Pasadena the road continues to Los Angeles, where it originally ended at Broadway and 7th Street. Wait a minute! Los Angeles? What about the Pacific Ocean? What about Santa Monica? What about the pier at sunset? Facing pressure to make Route 66 the tourist route to the Pacific Ocean, a proposal to extend the route was submitted to and approved by AASHTO (American Association of State Highway and Transportation Officials). On January 1, 1936, the end of the Mother Road was officially extended to Santa Monica, ending at the intersection of Lincoln and Olympic Boulevards (now an on-ramp to I-10).

ABOVE: *The Madonna of the Trail was dedicated by the Daughters of the American Revolution in February 1929 to honor the pioneer women who came West.* **RIGHT:** *The WigWam Motel in Rialto offers a classic place to spend the night while on the road.*

No one really knows why, but Route 66 ends eight short blocks from the ocean. But for the roadies of the world, the Mother Road ends at the Santa Monica Pier. So go ahead, follow Santa Monica Boulevard all the way to Ocean Avenue, go left one block, and then take your final right onto the pier. Park and walk to the end of the pier, and if it is sunset, and it really should be sunset, look out across the Pacific and think back upon the journey... You have traveled the Mother Road from Chicago to Los Angeles and experienced the ultimate road trip. You are now an official Roadie—wear the title well.

TOP: *The famous Hollywood sign stands above Route 66, which is now Santa Monica Blvd., in Los Angeles.* **ABOVE:** *Los Angeles Chinatown offers a variety of shopping and dining experiences in a colorful and entertaining atmosphere.* **RIGHT:** *The end of the journey. Although not an official part of Route 66, the Santa Monica Pier is the symbolic end of the Mother Road and what better time to experience it than at sunset.*

ON AND AROUND ROUTE 66: CALIFORNIA

NEEDLES
The El Garces Harvey House
Downtown between F and G Streets
760.326.5678
http://www.geocities.com/needleselgarces/
A classic Fred Harvey creation

BARSTOW
Barstow Route 66 Mother Road Museum
681 N. First Avenue, 760.255.1890,
http://barstow66museum.itgo.com/
A beautifully restored Harvey House now used by Greyhound and Amtrak

VICTORVILLE
California Route 66 Museum, 16825 D Street
760.951.0436, http://www.califrt66museum.org
A nice collection of historic photographs and artifacts related to the history of Route 66 and its communities in California

SAN BERNARDINO
San Bernardino Route 66 Museum
1398 N. E Street, 909.885.6324
www.wemweb.com/chr66a/sbr66_museum.html
Housed on the site of the original McDonald's, this museum pays homage to both SpeeDee, the McDonald's chef, and Route 66.

PASADENA
Norton Simon Museum
411 W. Colorado Blvd.
626.449.6840, www.nortonsimon.org
Art exhibits from the Renaissance through today

HOLLYWOOD

Grauman's Chinese Theatre
6925 Hollywood Blvd., 323.464.8111
Place your feet in the footprints of the stars (but don't pull a Lucy
and run away with a square!)

Hollywood Wax Museum
6767 Hollywood Blvd.
323.462.8860, www.hollywoodwax.com
Life-size figures of the stars and recreated sets from famous films
and TV shows

LOS ANGELES

Farmers Market
6333 W. 3rd Street
323.933.9211, www.farmersmarketla.com
An open-air market offering gourmet foods and unique
gift items, serving customers since 1934

Olvera Street
North of the Plaza between Main and Alameda Streets downtown
845 N. Alameda Street, 213.680.2525, www.olvera-street.com
Revitalized in 1930 as a classic Mexican marketplace
along one of the oldest streets in the city

Chinatown
Downtown, surrounded by Cesar Chavez, Spring, Yale, and
Bennett Streets
323.222.0856, www.chinatownla.com
Chinese shops, restaurants, and festivals take place along
Gin Ling Way, the street of Golden Treasures

Travel Town Museum
5200 Zoo Drive, 323.662.5874, www.ci.la.ca.us/RAP/grifmet/tt/
Outdoor transportation museum with steam locomotives and
classic rail cars, indoor area with auto exhibits

Petersen Automotive Museum
6060 Wilshire Blvd., 323.930.2277, www.petersen.org
Exhibits trace milestones in the development of the automobile
and Los Angeles

	Dwight	Bloomington	Springfield, IL	St. Louis	Rolla	Springfield, MO	Galena	Quapaw	Tulsa	Oklahoma City	El Reno	Sayre	Shamrock	Groom	Amarillo	Glenrio	Tucumcari	Santa Rosa	Santa Fe	Albuquerque	Grants	Gallup	Holbrook	Winslow	Flagstaff	Williams	Kingman	Needles	Barstow	San Bernardino	Los Angeles	Santa Monica
Chicago	78	135	201	303	408	517	598	606	696	801	827	927	964	1013	1061	1131	1172	1229	1393	1345	1420	1481	1576	1607	1665	1699	1812	1873	1963	2032	2076	2092
Dwight		58	123	220	331	440	521	529	619	724	749	849	887	936	979	1049	1090	1148	1255	1264	1338	1399	1494	1526	1584	1617	1731	1792	1936	2005	2050	2066
Bloomington	58		67	163	274	384	465	472	562	667	693	793	831	880	923	993	1033	1091	1198	1207	1281	1343	1441	1469	1527	1561	1674	1735	1878	1947	1992	2008
Lincoln	89	32	33	129	240	350	425	433	523	628	653	753	791	840	889	959	999	1057	1165	1174	1248	1309	1405	1436	1493	1527	1641	1701	1844	1913	1958	1976
Springfield, IL	123	67		98	203	313	388	401	491	596	622	722	760	809	858	927	971	1029	1214	1197	1271	1332	1427	1459	1465	1499	1612	1673	1816	1885	1929	1946
St. Louis	219	163	98		106	216	291	304	394	499	525	631	669	718	760	832	871	929	1038	1045	1119	1180	1275	1307	1361	1395	1507	1568	1711	1781	1824	1840
Rolla	331	274	203	106		203	187	200	290	395	421	521	559	607	651	720	760	819	926	935	1009	1070	1165	1197	1255	1288	1402	1463	1606	1675	1719	1735
Springfield, MO	440	384	313	216	203		84	91	181	286	312	413	450	499	541	612	653	711	818	826	901	962	1057	1088	1146	1179	1293	1354	1497	1566	1611	1629
Joplin	508	451	381	285	179	71	8	22	114	219	244	345	382	431	474	544	585	642	752	759	835	896	991	1023	1080	1113	1227	1288	1431	1500	1545	1563
Galena	521	465	388	291	187	84		94	185	290	316	416	378	427	470	540	581	639	747	755	830	892	987	1018	1076	1109	1223	1284	1427	1496	1541	1559
Quapaw	529	472	401	304	200	91	14		99	204	230	330	368	417	457	527	567	626	735	743	816	879	984	1006	1063	1096	1211	1271	1414	1483	1528	1547
Claremore	592	535	465	369	263	155	84	73	30	135	161	261	298	347	391	460	502	560	666	677	751	812	907	939	996	1029	1144	1204	1347	1416	1461	1479
Tulsa	619	562	491	394	290	181	109	99		107	133	233	271	320	363	433	474	533	640	649	723	784	879	911	969	1002	1116	1177	1320	1389	1433	1452
Oklahoma City	724	667	596	499	395	286	290	204	214		28	128	166	215	258	328	368	426	534	543	617	678	773	805	862	896	1010	1071	1214	1283	1327	1346
El Reno	749	692	622	527	421	312	241	231	133	28		104	141	190	234	304	344	402	510	518	593	654	748	780	838	871	985	1046	1189	1258	1302	1321
Clinton	804	748	678	588	477	368	297	287	189	84	60	45	82	131	174	245	285	343	450	459	533	594	689	721	779	812	926	987	1130	1199	1243	1262
Sayre	848	791	722	631	521	412	341	331	233	128	104		38	87	131	200	241	299	407	415	490	550	645	677	735	767	882	942	1086	1155	1199	1218
Shamrock	885	829	759	669	558	449	378	368	271	165	141	38		51	94	165	205	263	370	379	453	515	610	641	699	733	846	907	1050	1119	1164	1182
McLean	905	848	778	688	577	469	397	386	290	184	160	57	21	30	73	144	184	242	350	359	433	494	589	621	678	711	826	886	1029	1098	1143	1161
Groom	934	878	808	717	607	498	427	416	319	214	190	87	51		43	114	154	212	319	328	402	463	558	590	648	681	795	856	999	1068	1112	1131
Amarillo	979	922	852	761	651	542	471	460	363	258	234	131	94	43		72	112	171	278	287	361	422	517	549	607	639	754	815	958	1027	1071	1090
Glenrio	1048	991	926	830	720	611	540	530	432	327	304	200	165	114	72		43	102	209	218	292	353	448	480	538	571	685	746	889	958	1002	1021
Tucumcari	1089	1032	967	871	760	652	581	570	473	368	344	241	205	154	113	43		60	168	175	249	311	405	437	495	528	642	703	846	915	960	978
Santa Rosa	1146	1089	1025	929	818	709	639	628	530	425	402	299	262	211	171	102	60		108	117	191	252	347	379	437	470	584	645	788	857	901	934
Santa Fe	1255	1198	1133	1037	926	818	746	736	639	534	510	407	370	319	278	209	168	108		63	137	198	293	325	383	416	530	591	734	803	847	866
Albuquerque	1263	1206	1141	1045	934	826	755	745	647	542	518	415	379	328	287	218	175	117	63		77	138	233	265	323	356	470	531	674	743	787	806
Grants	1337	1281	1220	1120	1009	901	830	819	722	617	593	490	453	402	361	292	249	191	137	77		62	157	189	246	279	394	454	597	666	711	730
Gallup	1398	1341	1280	1180	1070	961	890	880	782	677	654	550	515	463	422	353	311	252	198	138	62		96	128	185	218	332	393	536	605	650	668
Holbrook	1493	1441	1375	1275	1164	1056	985	974	877	772	748	645	610	558	517	448	405	347	293	233	157	96		33	90	123	238	298	441	510	555	574
Winslow	1525	1468	1407	1308	1196	1088	1017	1006	909	804	780	677	641	590	549	480	437	379	325	265	189	128	33		58	91	205	266	409	478	522	541
Flagstaff	1583	1526	1465	1365	1254	1146	1074	1064	967	862	838	735	699	648	607	538	495	437	383	323	246	185	90	58		33	147	208	351	420	465	481
Williams	1615	1558	1497	1397	1287	1178	1107	1097	999	894	871	767	733	681	640	571	528	470	416	356	279	218	123	91	33		115	175	318	387	432	448
Seligman	1658	1601	1540	1440	1329	1221	1150	1139	1042	937	913	810	774	723	682	612	570	512	459	397	322	260	166	133	76	42	74	135	278	347	391	407
Kingman	1729	1673	1612	1512	1401	1293	1222	1211	1114	1009	958	882	846	856	815	746	703	645	591	531	454	393	298	266	208	175		62	205	274	319	335
Topock	1777	1721	1659	1560	1449	1341	1269	1259	1162	1057	1033	930	894	843	802	732	690	632	578	517	442	380	285	253	195	162	49	14	157	226	270	286
Needles	1790	1733	1672	1572	1462	1353	1282	1272	1174	1069	1046	942	907	856	815	746	703	645	591	531	454	393	298	266	208	175	62		144	213	257	274
Amboy	1864	1808	1745	1646	1535	1426	1355	1345	1248	1143	1119	1016	979	929	888	818	776	717	664	603	528	466	371	339	281	248	135	75	79	148	193	209
Ludlow	1882	1825	1764	1665	1554	1445	1374	1364	1266	1161	1138	1035	998	947	907	837	795	736	683	622	547	485	390	358	300	267	154	93	52	121	165	181
Barstow	1964	1877	1816	1716	1605	1497	1426	1415	1318	1213	1189	1086	1050	999	958	888	846	788	734	674	597	536	441	409	351	318	205	144		70	115	131
Victorville	1997	1910	1849	1749	1638	1530	1459	1448	1351	1246	1222	1119	1083	1032	991	922	880	821	768	706	631	596	475	442	385	352	239	177	35	37	81	98
San Bernardino	2032	1945	1884	1785	1674	1565	1494	1484	1387	1282	1258	1155	1118	1068	1027	957	915	857	803	743	666	605	510	478	420	387	274	213	70		59	75
Pasadena	2068	1981	1920	1820	1709	1601	1530	1519	1422	1317	1293	1190	1154	1103	1062	992	950	892	839	777	702	640	546	513	456	423	309	248	106	57	11	28
Los Angeles	2077	1990	1929	1829	1718	1610	1539	1528	1431	1326	1302	1199	1164	1112	1071	1002	960	901	847	787	711	650	555	522	465	432	319	257	115	59		16
Santa Monica	2093	2006	1944	1845	1734	1629	1557	1547	1450	1345	1321	1218	1182	1131	1090	1021	978	934	866	806	730	668	574	541	481	448	335	274	131	75	16	

All distances are estimated.